connections

liverpool: global gateway

Arabella McIntyre-Brown and Guy Woodland

garlic PRESS

A Liverpool-bound Sea Cat enters the mouth of the Mersey

connections

Written by Arabella McIntyre-Brown and Fiona Shaw
Portrait and faces photography by Guy Woodland

Design by Smiling Wolf
Layout by Garlic Press
Printed and bound in Spain by Bookprint SL

ISBN: 1-904099-08-4
A catalogue for this book is available from the British Library

First published in January 2005 by Garlic Press Publishing Ltd

Garlic Press Publishing Ltd
71 Prenton Road West, Birkenhead CH42 9PZ
Tel +44 (0)151 608 7006
email: connections@garlicpress.co.uk

www.garlicpress.co.uk

Many photographers have helped to build up the world picture, including:

Pippa Botting
Nick Botting
John Chalinor
Fred Chan
Kevin Dwyer
Robert Harding
Jeremy Horner/Panos
Angela Hurren
Failte Ireland
Tetsushi Kobayashi
David Lindley
Sue Lindley
Arabella McIntyre-Brown
Paul McMullin
Garry Owen
Marc Schlossman/Panos
Jersey Tourism
Guy Woodland

Thanks also to the British Institute of Professional Photography members, who have been a great help.

contents

Beetham Tower makes its mark on the Liverpool skyline

foreword

Hugh Frost

The location of the Beetham Tower in Liverpool, from which you can see out to Liverpool Bay, the Irish Sea, and beyond, was the genesis of the idea of the garden representing Liverpool as a global gateway. Looking out over the River Mersey, which has spawned so many great enterprises and seen so many people carried in and out of the city on the tide, one can only try to imagine the excitement and trepidation of passengers, crew and masters facing an uncertain future.

For the early explorers of trade routes, setting out on the vast and turbulent Atlantic in vulnerable little wooden ships, it was a lottery whether they would even survive the journey, let alone bring home a profitable cargo.

Those who embarked on long and often dangerous voyages in search of political freedom, economic fortune, or simply a new life in a new world, were stepping into the unknown with everything they possessed. It took courage and commitment when common sense probably suggested that there was a safer option.

At Beetham we believe wholeheartedly in Liverpool's renaissance and we are thoroughly committed to its success. The Beetham Organization is a company that has grown in Liverpool; the family has long connections here, and the business has grown with the city's regeneration. From time to time we have had to take the leap of faith against received wisdom.

The built environment is vital to the life of the city, but the heart and the lifeblood of every company, and every city, is its people. And Liverpool's people are at the heart of this book and the garden project.

Readers of this book will meet the Faces of Liverpool to be found in the garden; read their stories, and through these 32 people living in the city in 2005, will get a flavour of the city's past and present in all its richness and variety. Each story, while intensely personal, is typical of many other people's experience, and the whole collection builds up a portrait of Liverpool through the lives of its citizens.

For Beetham to have the opportunity to sponsor such a special public art project is a source of great pride to my company, and we are delighted that this book both commemorates the garden project and increases our knowledge and appreciation of Liverpool's place on the world stage.

BEETHAM

East meets West: a Buddhist monk in Thailand

introduction

Arabella McIntyre-Brown

Centuries before records began, the area we know as Liverpool has been a point of arrival and departure. People have washed in and out of the Mersey on the tide, from every corner of the globe, creating a vibrant and diverse gene pool, a trading history and a record of innovation that is one of the richest in the world.

Neolithic boat people left the Calder Stones as their lasting mark; Celts, Scots, Vikings, Saxons are remembered in names and blood lines. National identities linger in local communities: Yemen, Ireland, Greece, China, France, Chile, Spain, Poland, Norway, Somalia, Kosovo. Memories of language, food, fabrics, songs and customs have been woven into the pattern of Liverpool life for so many centuries that the city is hard to classify. Certainly not English, not even British, the worldwide inspiration of Liverpool's culture (in its widest sense) makes this an exciting, complicated, temperamental, often infuriating place to live.

There are those who, with stunning ignorance of their history and equally stunning bigotry, demand querulously that Liverpool should belong to Liverpudlians, and that all who are not true Scousers should be repatriated.

Define 'Liverpudlian'. Who is a true Scouser? How far back must one trace one's ancestry to stake a claim?

The city was created from a few square miles of marshy coastline that was fit for nothing but fishing until a Frenchman – a Norman king – realised that it would be a convenient place to ferry his army to and from Ireland. It has always been foreigners who saw and exploited the potential of this area; the ancient Britons didn't make a good job of hanging on in here, after all.

The modern Liverpudlian has a genetic audit trail so complicated that racism, let alone nationalism, is an ironic irrelevance. It still thrives, though, to a degree that is not only shameful but stupid.

Some of the most enterprising people in this city are marginalised and their talent and energy wasted. This is a hole below the waterline of the good ship Regeneration; it may not capsize it, but it's doing damage.

As for those who have come here as refugees – the few that have been allowed to stay – their passion to make good lives for themselves and their families, their hunger for education, their energy, self-sufficiency, fresh ideas, ambition and drive is exactly what Liverpool and Merseyside needs in container loads.

In the third millennium AD, invaders don't turn up armed with swords and clubs, but with laptops and mobiles, looking for knowledge and profit. Some students might look as shaggy as their prehistoric forebears, but are generally more benign (except perhaps at chucking out time in Concert Square).

The nearest thing to a Viking horde these days is a bunch of Geordies after a win at Goodison Park. Woe betide any maidens in town then. On the other hand, woe betide a love-lorn Geordie trying to find a maiden. He's more likely to get eaten alive by the descendants of Valkyries and Amazons that live round these parts.

This book offers only a taste of the many flavours that make up the cultural feast that is Liverpool.

The city's history is reflected, and its future created, in the rainbow of faces here, and in the stories they have to tell.

Cunard: traditional transporter of people, hopes and dreams, to and from Liverpool

chapter one
global gateway

europe

Europeans were colonising Liverpool long before records began. Iron Age Celts made this their home and defended it when the Romans marched up the A5; although the Romans didn't fancy the marsh on the east side of the Mersey – they built their fort at Chester (Deva) as a base from which to keep the Celtic Brigantes under control.

Once the Romans quit Britain and headed home for sun, olives and Falernian red wine, it was centuries before another Italian community was established in the city, but in the meantime the Germans and Scandinavians arrived. And then the French made their mark, with the arrival in England of the Duke of Normandy, aka William the Conqueror. Liverpool is not mentioned in the 1086 audit of the Normans' new kingdom, but Toxteth and West Derby are there. The first mention of Liverpool is in a deed signed by the Norman Prince John in 1190, making a present of the area to his falconer. Seventeen years later, now king, John signed the town's first charter in 1207 (still in the city's archives).

Liverpool's royal charter of 1556 was signed by the King of Spain, oddly enough: Philip II was the husband of the English Queen Mary I, and both signed the charter.

Philip didn't remain a friend; 32 years later he sent the Spanish Armada across the Channel. It is said to have been a Liverpool privateer, Humphrey Brooke, who discovered his plans and reported them to Francis Drake, busy playing bowls on Plymouth Hoe.

By the beginning of the 17th century Liverpool was importing and exporting a wide variety of goods. Salt herrings and

At sea on the Mediterranean: Europe meets Africa

Liverpool's royal charter of 1556 was signed by the King of Spain, oddly enough – Philip II was the husband of English Queen Mary I, and both signed the charter

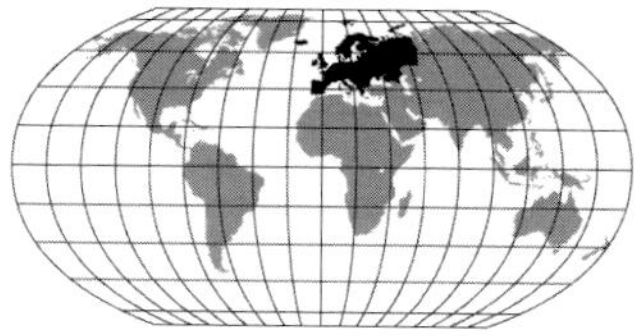

salt beef, sheepskins, tallow, linen, flax, frieze and mantles were among the goods coming in from Europe, and Liverpool was in turn exporting goods including copper, iron, coal, hops, alum, soap and Yorkshire cloth.

Among the local merchants who had begun to import goods were Edward and Thomas Tarleton who, during the 1590s, extended the import of Spanish iron from Bilbao which had been begun by Christopher Crosse some 30 years before. The Williamson family, whose business was in leather, shoes and tanning, got skins and hides from France, Spain and Ireland. Another leading Liverpool family, the Norris family, traded with Bordeaux in France, Spain and Turkey. The Slaughterhouse pub in Fenwick Street was built during the reign of George III by wine merchants importing from France, Spain and Portugal.

Profits were not only made on good trading relationships. For several centuries Liverpool mariners made handsome fortunes from privateering – little more than licensed piracy. Queen Elizabeth I started the practice, giving letters of marque to favoured sea dogs, allowing them to raid and seize foreign ships in international waters. French and Spanish prizes brought huge wealth to Liverpool's shipowners, with a single captured ship worth, quite literally, a king's ransom.

One such was a French Eastindiaman, the *Carnatic*, which was captured by the *Mentor*, a ship owned by shipwright Peter Baker. Baker had built the *Mentor* but failed to sell her, so put a crew on board under a Captain Dawson, and became a privateer. The *Carnatic* proved to be a very rich prize, and Baker built himself the grand Mossley Hall, immediately nicknamed Carnatic Hall. The house didn't survive, but the name stuck, and is now the Carnatic halls of residence of the University of Liverpool.

The Napoleonic Wars saw about 4,000 French prisoners of war brought to Liverpool and incarcerated in the Tower of Liverpool, next to St Nicholas parish church. Over 200 of them died there, and many escaped; when the survivors were eventually released, many stayed in the town, found wives and settled here.

The French who died were buried in the churchyard of St John's church; the site is now St John's Gardens, below St George's Hall, and there is a memorial to the French who are buried there.

A happier association with France is through Edouard André, a leading landscape architect and horticulturist. At the age of 20 he was appointed head gardener of the City of Paris, and was a member of the team that laid out the parks and boulevards that transformed Paris into a model modern city. His Liverpool connection was as designer – with Lewis Hornblower – of Sefton Park. The pair won the competition to design the park in 1866, and spent £146,000 on its creation.

There was a Roman camp in Woolton, and remains of a Roman road were found at Otterspool and in Grassendale.

The statue on the top of the Wellington Memorial is said to be made from a French cannon captured at the Battle of Waterloo.

During World War 2, fuel was pumped from the River Mersey all the way to the Normandy beaches through PLUTO: the Pipe Line Under The Ocean. Its Merseyside terminal was at Dingle Point.

Old Swan was at one time a centre for glassmaking; a large glassworks at the top of Edge Lane employed 40 French experts.

The University of Liverpool established the first Chair of Spanish, in 1908, and its Department of Iberian and Latin Studies is renowned for excellence.

Liverpool clockmaker Sewills has been in business since 1800; the name Sewill is believed to derive from Sephardic Jews who came to Liverpool from Seville. The firm was appointed clockmaker to the Queen of Spain in 1862, the same year that Napoleon III awarded Sewills a gold medal at the Paris Exhibition. In 1869 Sewills made a chronometer for the *Cutty Sark* for the great Tea Races from China, and its chronometers were installed in Royal Navy ships such as *Ark Royal* and *HMS Belfast*.

europe

When the brilliant 19th century astronomer William Lassell found the skies over Liverpool too cloudy and polluted, he took his revolutionary 24-inch telescope to Malta, in 1852. The island's latitude, mild climate and transparent night skies were the envy of his British colleagues. Lassell's expedition to Malta opened the eyes of northern European astronomers to what are called 'prime sky locations' for big telescopes.

Many Liverpool ships have ended their days in the seas around Europe: *Ann Paley*, *George IV* and *Rosalind* were lost off the Iberian coast. The ships *Italian* and *Syrian* were both lost in fog off Cape Finisterre in 1869. *Sarah* and *Mary* were both seized by the French in 1810 – *Mary* was then sold in Jamaica.

Football is a key trade for Liverpool these days: Liverpool FC's manager – Spaniard Rafael Benitez – was preceded by Frenchman Gerard Houllier. 2004 players such as Djibril Cissé (French) and Xavi Alonso (Spanish), club captain Sami Hyypia (Finnish) succeed famous European names of the past. Scandinavia has produced many fine players for Merseyside, such as 1980s Liverpool star Jan Molby and Everton's highly-rated Thomas Gravesen – both from Denmark.

St Patrick preached a sermon in Liverpool on his journey to Ireland in 432AD; he was shipwrecked.

Silkhouse Court, the office block in Tithebarn Street, is on the site of Liverpool's first factory – a silk factory run by Italian silk manufacturers. A steady flow of Italians came to Liverpool between 1880 and 1912; they worked as organ-grinders, street entertainers, musicians, knife-sharpeners and hotel staff – and notably as ice cream-makers. The streets around Scotland Road became Little Italy – by 1913 there were more than 400 Italian-born residents there, but in the slum clearances of the 1930s, most of these little streets were razed and their inhabitants rehoused.

Boxing was a hugely popular sport, of course, and one of Little Italy's celebrities was Dom Volante, born to Italian parents in Gerard Street, and later a world-class boxer who topped the bill at Madison Square Gardens in New York.

The Greek and Cypriot community, now about 2,000 strong, began in 1810 with shipowners and traders (George Papayannis founded the Ellerman & Papayannis line here in 1855) and in 1871 there were about 300 Greeks here: the families of merchants here to deal in the corn and cotton trade for the Mediterranean area. At the start of the 1900s most of the wealthy Greek families migrated to Australia or America, and it wasn't until British soldiers brought Greek brides home from World War 2, and the Cypriots came over in the 1960s, that the community began to thrive and prosper.

Liverpool's Greek Orthodox Church, at the top of Princes Road, was consecrated in 1870 by the Archbishop of Syra & Tinos, in the presence of the Archbishops of York and Canterbury. The eight pillars of marble are from Mount Pentelion, the same source as the marble of the Parthenon in Athens. The icons are also Greek originals, and the three hour service is still conducted, in Greek, as it has been for 2,000 years.

From the home nations, Liverpool has drawn millions over the centuries.

The Welsh came to Liverpool in droves; the first Welsh chapel was built in Pall Mall in 1787; the community grew so large that Pall Mall became known as Little Wales and, in 1788, a Liverpool Welsh penny was minted. (Place names like Walton and Wallasey suggest that Welsh Celts may have arrived here in the first millennium AD.) By 1813, one in ten people in Liverpool were Welsh and over the next 40 years Welsh numbers grew from 8,000 to 40,000; many spoke no English – in Everton and Kirkdale local newspapers were in Welsh. There were even six National Eisteddfod held here – in 1840, 1855, 1884, 1900 1903 and 1929.

As for the Scots, they came to prosper. Medics, scholars, engineers, merchants – famous names such as Gladstone and Laird, for example. By 1837, there were enough Scots to support six congregations (the ruined Scottish church of St Andrew is in Rodney Street) and they prospered in

By 1845 the Welsh numbered 40,000; in Everton and Kirkdale local newspapers were in Welsh. There were even six National Eisteddfod held in Liverpool

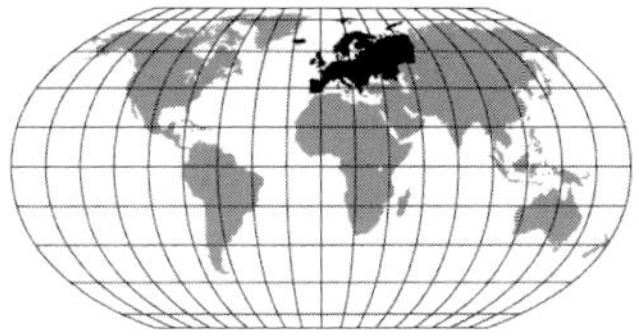

ship-building, rope-making, engineering and sugar-refining.

The Irish have made Liverpool their home for centuries (Freemen of Liverpool were Freemen of Waterford and Wexford too). The Irish influence on Liverpool has been enormous, from the accent to politics, literature and music.

Migration and trade across the Irish Sea started pre-history, but it wasn't until the 19th century that the Irish flood began. In 1819 their numbers were high enough to spark Orange and Green riots in the city. (In 1881 there was a Fenian attempt to blow up the Town Hall with dynamite.)

The potato famine in the 1840s drove two million people (a quarter of Ireland's population) across the treacherous Irish Sea to Liverpool, in 'coffin ships', many of whom sailed on to the New World. But in Mulberry Street is a blue plaque: 'Near this place in 1847 some 2,600 destitute Irish Famine migrants were buried in unmarked pauper graves. They had died in extreme poverty in the parish of Liverpool, so ending their flight from the Great Hunger 1845–52.'

Two women from Ireland are famous in Liverpool, for very different reasons.

Kitty Wilkinson, the 'saint of the streets', came from Londonderry; in 1833, when cholera hit Liverpool, she worked ceaselessly to keep the poor free of the disease, and helped get the country's first public baths and wash-houses built.

Margaret Kelly was born in Dublin but grew up in Liverpool and made her stage debut here. She is better known as Miss Bluebell – her troupe of dancers, the Bluebell Girls, were the toast of Paris, and Miss Bluebell was a heroine to the French in World War 2. She died in 2004.

The Rock of Gibraltar: gateway to the Mediterranean

Sunrise over the Cheshire plain

europe

Some of the earliest documents on Merseyside are the Viking records dating back to 902AD, when a group of settlers, led by Ingimund, won permission from Alfred the Great's daughter, Queen Aethelflaed, to build a community on the Wirral (with Thingwall at its heart). Farmers and fishermen, they were still Vikings, and five years later, in 907 they invaded Chester and sailed across the River Mersey to found communities in Toxteth, Garston, Crosby, West Derby and Kirkby.

Further evidence is provided by the hoard of coins found in Crosby, from the reign of Danil Gulfrith, King of Northumbria in 883.

Much later, Liverpool mariners ventured north into Scandinavian waters, trading along the coast and whaling. In Greenland is an area of spectacular beauty called Liverpool Land: glaciers, fjords, hot springs, icebergs and mountains. Many ships have been wrecked in the pack ice. Close by is Rathbone Island – named after a famous Liverpool family.

The Norwegian and Swedish community in Liverpool has its own church, the Seaman's Church dedicated to Gustav Adolf, in Park Lane. Opened in 1884, its distinctive design is by the architect Caroe, who was the son of the Danish consul.

Arguably one of the most crucial marks left by the Scandinavians on Liverpudlian culture is Scouse. Brought to Liverpool by northern European seamen, Lobscouse – or Labskaus – was a quick, cheap and filling hash of beef, onion and potatoes. Not exactly Wiener Schnitzel or Salade Niçoise, but it hit the spot with cold and hungry sailors.

Lions guarding the Louvre, Paris

In 1951 the number of Mormon migrants was an astonishing 85,000, including the father and grandfather of Western outlaw Butch Cassidy

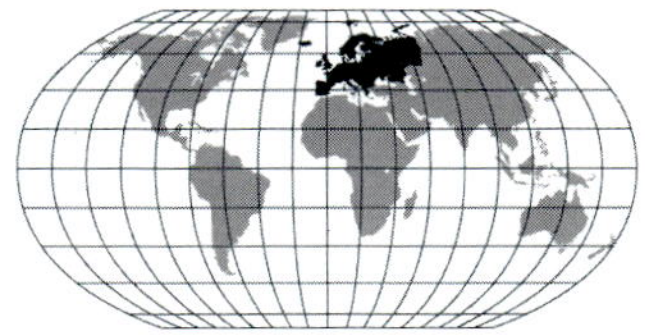

One group of Scandinavians began a great religious migration, in 1851, which went on for decades. The American Church of Jesus Christ of the Latter Day Saints – Mormons – sent missionaries to Europe, setting up an emigration agency in Liverpool. Missionaries arrived in Norway on 11 September and despite widespread opposition began to recruit converts. The church encouraged converts to move to Utah, where they would be free to practise their religion.

The journey was long and arduous; despite being shepherded by church elders the migrants often met opposition.

A group of 200 Norwegian migrants in 1863, for instance, left home on 13 April to travel to Christiania, then by steamship to Copenhagen and on to Kiel. Then they crossed Germany by train to Hamburg, where they boarded another ship for Hull or Grimsby. Then overland by train to Liverpool, where they arrived on 6 May. Here the Norwegian migrants joined Mormons from all over Scandinavia – 681 in all; they boarded the ship *Kimball*, bound for New York and the long overland journey to Salt Lake City.

In 1849 some 2,500 Mormons sailed from Liverpool; in 1951 the number of migrants was an astonishing 85,000, including the father and grandfather of outlaw Butch Cassidy. To mark the 150th anniversary of this great migration, the Mormon Church gave a statue to the city of Liverpool in 2001.

Religious migrants – this time Jewish refugees – flooded into Liverpool from Russia, Poland, Germany and central Europe, both in the 1880s and in the war-torn 20th century.

The first influx began in October 1881, when refugees began their long flight to North America.

In March 1881, Russian Tsar Alexander II was assassinated and, as one of the six conspirators was Jewish, Russian fury was vented on the Jews. Pogroms began in Odessa at Easter and spread to 200 Russian towns and cities; Jews fled to Brody, a town on the Polish/Russian border (now in Ukraine) with a large Jewish population. By May 1882, there were 12,000 refugees in Brody – almost 50% of the existing population.

To help manage the chaos in the overcrowded town, a French organisation, Alliance Israelite Universelle, set up in Brody to help the thousands who wanted to travel to Liverpool, via Hamburg and Hull; here they were looked after by the local branch of the Anglo-Jewish Association, and their passage to America or Canada arranged.

The Liverpool Commission provided tickets for the sea passage and trains; refugees were met on arrival in America and helped on their way to their final destination. Between 27 April and 12 July 1882 over 6,000 Brody refugees travelled to North America, on 31 ships, at a total cost of £30,000.

An authentic old German recipe for Labskaus calls for salt beef or corned beef, lots of onions, and potatoes. Cooked to rags, the meat and onions are mixed into the mashed potato and eaten with pickled cucumber.

Today's Liverpool recipe for Scouse has been rather influenced by Irish Stew, and has turned into a soupy stew of mutton (or lamb), potatoes, onions, carrots and whatever other veg is available. For even cheaper or 'blind' Scouse, leave out the meat. Eat your bowl of Scouse with pickled red cabbage or pickled beetroot.

The Royal Liverpool Philharmonic Orchestra has had a long association with northern and eastern European musicians, from composers Alfred Schnittke and Max Bruch to conductors Sir Charles Hallé, Walter Weller, Marek Janowski, Libor Pesek and Petr Altrichter.

One of the most distinguished scientists of the 20th century is Joseph Rotblat, the Polish physicist who was awarded the Nobel Peace Prize in 1995 for his work as secretary-general of the Pugwash Conferences. Coming to Liverpool University in 1939, Rotblat worked with Sir James Chadwick on the atomic bomb, first in Liverpool, then on the Manhattan Project in Los Alamos. In 1955 he chaired the press conference which announced the Russell-Einstein Manifesto.

europe

Liverpool names such as Aigburth (grove of oaks), Bootle (*botl* = village), Smithdown (or *Esmedune*) and Calderstones (*galdar* = wizard) are evidence of the city's Saxon occupation.

In the *Domesday Book* of 1086, Esmedune is noted as being worth 32 pennies to its Saxon landlord, Aethelmund. In 1204, King John was creating his Toxteth hunting park and, wanting more land, bought Esmedune from Richard, son of Thurstan. In return, this Saxon landlord was given the Thingwall estate on the Wirral.

Liverpool's Hahnemann Hospital was named after the German inventor of homeopathy, Dr Samuel Hahnemann.

Sugar-refining – a key industry in Liverpool for centuries – was heavy, hot and dangerous work. English workers didn't fancy it, so from the 17th century on, German workers were recruited; pay was high, especially for skilled sugar-boilers, and beer was provided to rehydrate bodies working in the intense heat. In the 1851 census there were 44 German-born sugar workers in Liverpool; by 1881 there were about 200.

John Phillips (Johannes Philippi), born in Hesse-Darmstadt, came to Liverpool in the 1840s to work first as a sugar boiler, then by 1871 as foreman, possibly at Jager's refinery (owned by a German).

Liverpool's connections with Germany date back more than 1,000 years, to when the Saxons and Angles spread from the south and east coasts of England to colonise the marshy fishing coast of the North West.

The next notable influx from Germany to Liverpool began in the 18th century; from 1709 refugees from the Palatine (in southern Germany) had come to Liverpool and been settled in Sir Thomas's Buildings. Entries in Gore's Liverpool Directories include German merchants Meyer, Beyendorff, Lorentz, Zinck and the firm of Fuhrer & Wagner.

Towards the end of the century, records begin to show Jewish names such as Rabbi Benedict Yates (originally Baruch Goetz; he is also recorded as attending two Jews hanged at Chester in 1776 for robbery). The Yates family, descended through Benedict's brother Samuel, is well known in Liverpool's Jewish community.

In the community's archives, there is a list of 90 middle class Jews born before 1781, of whom at least 22 were born in Germany. But tracking Jewish immigrants is made difficult by the number of people who anglicised their names.

Jews came from Germany to England to improve their economic prospects, of course, but also because in England they would be free. In 18th century Germany Jews were often segregated, forced to wear badges, not allowed to learn certain crafts, and in some places only one son in the family was allowed to marry. In England, a Jew had most of the rights of any Englishman – he could vote in local elections (although until 1858 he could not stand as a candidate) and join the armed forces.

In the 19th and 20th centuries, sporadic tides of refugees from Germany and elsewhere in northern and eastern Europe made for Liverpool as the gateway to the New World – and some stayed here.

How ironic, then, that one of history's greatest authors of human suffering should have come to Liverpool himself, allegedly fleeing prosecution, if not persecution. It has long been an urban legend in Liverpool that art student Adolf Hitler was an habitué of certain city pubs. But now it seems that it might be true.

Certainly it is a matter of record that Alois Hitler, the elder half-brother of Adolf, married an Irish girl, Bridget Dowling, and settled in Liverpool, where Alois ran a hotel and a boarding house. The Hitlers lived at 102 Upper Stanhope Street, Toxteth, and in 1911 had a son, William Patrick.

The story goes that in 1912 Adolf, then aged 23 with artistic ambitions, had tried to avoid national service in Austria and fled the country before the police caught up with him. He came to his half-brother in England and is supposed to have stayed in Liverpool for about six months.

There is little evidence for claims that Alois was involved in spying for the

It has long been an urban legend in Liverpool that art student Adolf Hitler was an habitué of certain city pubs. But now it seems that it might be true

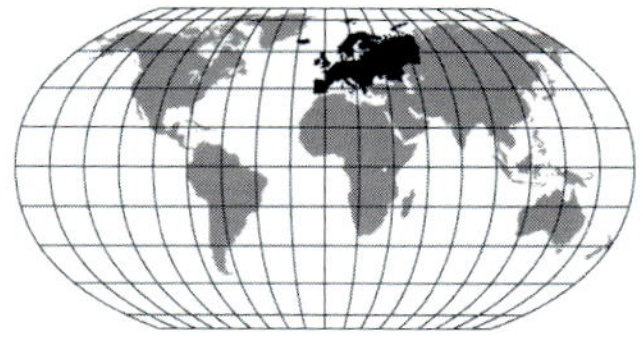

Austrians in the run-up to World War 1, but when his business went bust, Alois left his family and debunked to Germany.

In the 1930s, Liverpool-born William Hitler went to Germany to exploit his family connections. According to Bridget Hitler's memoirs, her son was not satisfied with the clerical job found for him by his father. William apparently suggested that unless something more fitting for the Fuhrer's nephew was offered to him, he would go public with stories that the self-proclaimed messiah of the Aryan peoples had a Jewish grandfather. Hitler ordered his nephew to renounce British citizenship and take a post in the Third Reich; William chose to go back to England but in 1939 it was not a place for a man called Hitler, so William and his mother sailed to New York, where he died in 1987.

Whatever the truth of his 1912 visit, there's no doubt of Hitler's impact on Liverpool during World War 2. The May Blitz, when so much of the city was flattened, was a result of Liverpool's key role as the centre of operations for the Battle of the Atlantic and left terrible scars on the fabric of the city and its people.

In an attempt to heal the wounds, a group of Liverpool's civic leaders went to Cologne in 1949 with the Anglo-German Friendship Society; three years later, in 1952, the two ports, on the Mersey and the Rhine, became twin cities in one of the earliest examples of such international partnerships. Fifty years ago, rebuilding trust between Germany and England was the priority. Now, in a unified Europe, where Liverpool will be the Capital of Culture in 2008, the twin cities must not forget the painful past which, for the older generation, is still very much alive.

Puerto Banus: a more traditional holiday spot than Toxteth?

asia & pacific rim

As well as being the main gateway to the Americas, Liverpool saw more emigrants leave for Australia and New Zealand than any other British port.

Not all went willingly. Among the 717 convicts on the first fleet of 11 ships that left England for Australia on 13 May 1787 were five from Liverpool (Mary MacCormack, William Murphy, William Parr, William Smith and John Roberts) and three from Ormskirk (William Allen, Peter Ellam and William Hindley).

Incidentally, six of the seven cattle brought out with the first fleet were found by a convict in the Cowpasture Road region of what is now the city of Liverpool, a suburb of Sydney. The six had increased to 60 when Governor Hunter visited the site in 1795, and he named it Cow Pasture Plains.

The town of Liverpool was founded on 7 November 1810 by Governor Lachlan Macquarie and named in honour of the Earl of Liverpool, then Secretary of State for the Colonies. Today it is one of the most multicultural cities in Australia, with thriving Fijian, Italian, Lebanese, Indian, Vietnamese and British communities.

In 1851 emigration was a different story. News of big gold discoveries in New South Wales and Victoria spurred a mad rush from all over Europe, and many thousands made their way to Liverpool to board steamships for the three- to five-month sea journey round the world.

From Wales, for instance, there were special emigrant trains every Monday from the valleys, attracted by advertisements from emigration agents. These agents had a variable reputation; in the 1870s one agent, Gomer Roberts, would promise only that he would '1) meet his

Sunrise over Melbourne

People have been swapping terrible tales of the horrors of Sydney – dirt, heat, vicious animals, robbers and illness – I don't know what to believe

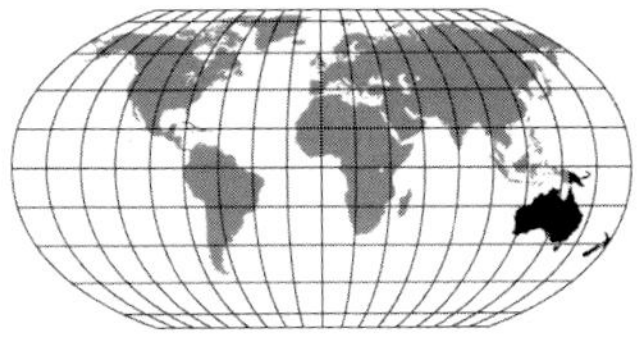

customers sober and 2) make sure they got on the right boat.'

There were emigration agents in Liverpool – such as Noah Jones and Eliasur Roberts – who were highly respected members of the Liverpool Welsh community; deacons in the chapels, or involved in the local eisteddfodau (Liverpool had a long established and self-contained Welsh community).

Many who went to Australia were on assisted passages – where either an employer in Australia looking for workers, the British government or the colonial government would pay their fares and a small allowance to help them get established. For the British government it was often cheaper to help a poor family to emigrate than to pay the poor relief.

Since either the taxpayer or a landowner had invested in these souls, they had an interest in getting them to Australia in good health and fit to work, to ensure some return from their investment.

Even so, travelling steerage was hard, with little space, no privacy and no escape from disease – many died of fever.

John Hedges migrated to Sydney in 1858 when he was 31, sailing from Birkenhead on the *Admiral Lyons* with his wife, Harriet and their sons, Walter and Basil. In his diary/letter to his mother John recorded the details of the voyage. These are his first impressions of Sydney:

'Since sighting land people have been swapping terrible tales of the horrors of Sydney – dirt, heat, vicious animals, robbers and illness. I don't know what to believe, but with Basil's illness in my thoughts I am all the more worried. At this moment I wish I'd never left London.'

The night before the ship docked, his two-year-old son Basil died of fever.

'The wind and waves took us backwards and forwards, and it took us hours to dock. We eventually arrived in Sydney after 81 days. From the ship it looked a rather small, hilly, and quite ugly looking town, with short bare trees and rocks. I later learnt that there are some good, clean streets, buildings and a post office.

'People rushed to leave the ship – as if a minute saved now will make a difference. On shore there was confusion, joy and sadness – unlike some others we have no one to welcome us to this new land. People wander, looking as lost as they did in Liverpool. I will find the agent's office and seek a place to bury my son.

'We have been on Australian soil for three days. Sydney is a pleasant town but very dusty. Many streets have English-sounding names. Goods are very expensive but are of reasonable quality, and meat is fairly cheap so we do not starve.

'I have seen some of our fellow passengers since we arrived. They've not found work – and some would have returned to Britain on the ship but for the fact it's already departed. I am tired and sad and can hardly bring myself to think about finding employment.'

Liverpool is Australia's fourth oldest town behind Sydney, Parramatta and Hobart. But unlike these cities, Liverpool was the first free planned settlement of Australia.
The coming of the railway, opened in September 1856 and the electric telegraph, in 1858, began the transformation of Liverpool into a major regional city.
The First World War brought changes to Liverpool. There were extensive military training activities in the area and German prisoners of war were held at Holsworthy.
Liverpool's current population is over 155,000. By 2020, 250,000 people are expected to call Liverpool home.

The coat of arms of Liverpool, New South Wales, reflects its relationship to Merseyside. The cormorant in the shield is taken from the arms of the city of Liverpool, but instead of seaweed, the bird holds in its beak a spray of wattle, the floral emblem of Australia.

In 1822, when Governor Macquarie left the colony, he commented that when he first came to Liverpool in 1810 it was a thick forest; but it now contained 'a handsome neat brick-built church, a brick-built hospital, a provision store, barrack, school-house, parsonage house, gaol and several other government buildings'. He also mentioned 'a wooden wharf or quay, in the centre of town, to which vessels of 50 tons can come to load and unload, which trade from Sydney to Liverpool, by way of Botany Bay'.

The dreaming spires of Hong Kong

LIPPO

asia & pacific rim

For over 200 years, until the early 19th century, trade with Asia was dominated by the London-based East India Company, so Liverpool merchants were baulked of the potential of the Far East until the EIC's monopoly was broken – in India in 1830, and three years later in China. Sir John Gladstone's ship *Kingsmill* was the first to India in search of a new source of cotton; and on 12 June 1834 the *Duchess of Clarence*, belonging to Liverpool line John Bibby & Co, was the first ship from China to arrive in the River Mersey. Her cargo was tea, and on board was a crew of Chinese sailors – it was the beginning of Europe's oldest Chinese community, here in Liverpool.

The same year, the *Symmetry* sailed from Liverpool to Guangzhou (Canton) with a cargo of cotton goods; from then on trade with China and the rest of Asia grew fast, particularly after the Suez Canal opened in 1869.

Out from Liverpool would go building materials, pottery, all kinds of manufactured goods, railway engines and track. A surveyor, Thomas Brassey, born in Birkenhead in 1805, began building roads, before moving on to the new fangled railways. He won an unparalleled reputation as a railway contractor globally, across Europe, Canada, Australia and India. The earliest British export to the East was Lancashire cotton fabric, but by the 1960s consumer goods, food, drink and cars were heading east from Liverpool.

Back from the Far East came silk and cotton, tea, spices, rice, hemp, jute. At the start of the 20th century Malaya was a key trading partner, exporting rubber, tobacco, sugar, tea and coffee to the UK.

From the 1850s, migrants were leaving from Liverpool to start new lives in Australia and New Zealand – and the ships returned with empty holds. Companies could improve profits by returning via India and China and loading the holds with high value goods. Later, Australian and New Zealand wool would be a valuable trade.

Albert Dock was Liverpool's key unloading dock for Asian route shipping, with good natural light and ventilation, being the first dock warehouses built out

Lake Pukaki and Mount Cook, Mount Cook National Park
South Island, New Zealand

A vain, self-centred man, tight with his money and more interested in his nudist and voyeuristic activities than in learning anything about authentic witchcraft

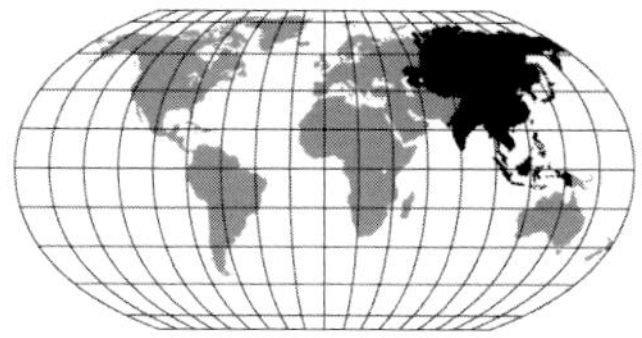

of non-combustible materials to cut the risk of fire; and being bonded warehouses gave the import/export merchants a significant financial advantage.

Many of Liverpool's shipping companies had some involvement in Asian trade – lines such as Brocklebank, Bibby, Holt and Clay exported millions of tons of finished goods from the Midlands and the North via Birkenhead, which specialised in handling bulky cargoes.

The *Corea*, a 581-ton full-rigged ship registered in 1859 to Liverpool firm Bushby & Edwards, was a fairly typical Liverpool clipper. One journey to Hong Kong and Whampoa began on 22 May 1865, when the *Corea* left Princes Dock with a crew comprised of master, three mates, bosun, carpenter, sail-maker, cook, steward, 12 ABs, two OSs and six apprentices. (One of the Able Seamen was lost overboard after falling from the rigging.) The outward voyage took the *Corea* past Madeira, Tenerife, Tristan de Cunha, Christmas Island, Java, Sumatra and Borneo before reaching Hong Kong on 7 September – a passage of 107 days. The *Corea* then sailed on to Foochow to load a cargo of tea, anchoring among famous tea clippers such as *Taeping*, *Fiery Cross* and *Belted Will* (another Bushby & Edwards clipper).

One of the fastest ever voyages from China to England was made by Liverpool clipper the *Scawfell*, owned by Rathbone Brothers. She could carry a cargo of just over a million pounds of tea (about 500 metric tons). A wooden full-rigged ship built in 1858, the *Scawfell* under Captain Robert Thomson left the Canton River on 14 January 1861 and arrived off Point Lynas, bound for Liverpool, on 11 April (85 days pilot to pilot).

Not all ships made it safely home, of course. The clipper *Friar Tuck*, bringing a cargo of tea back to Liverpool, was wrecked off the Scilly Isles in November 1863; her 22-strong crew was saved, but the islanders managed to acquire large quantities of tea despite the best efforts of coastguards. A lasting memorial to the *Friar Tuck* are the Chinese geese still thriving on Tresco, descendants of those which came ashore from the wreck.

The Liverpool shipping company most associated with the Far East, particularly China, is the Blue Funnel Line.

George Holt – of Lamport & Holt – had two sons, Albert and Philip: the brothers were confident technical innovators, and saw the founding of their own shipping line as the greatest adventure of their lives. Alfred Holt registered the Ocean Steamship Company in 1865, and their first ship – the *Agamemnon* – sailed from Liverpool on 19 April 1866: the first steamship ever to forge a link between Britain and the Far East.

The 2,280-ton sister ships with their distinctive blue funnels, *Agamemnon*, *Ajax* and *Achilles* (to the Holt brothers, Homer's Odyssey was the greatest adventure story

The man who links Liverpool, Malaya and witchcraft is Gerald Brosseau Gardner, born on 13 June 1884 in Blundellsands. His father was a merchant and a justice of the peace; Gerald's grandfather is said to have married a witch; certainly several of his forebears were Mayors of Liverpool.

After his education, Gardner went to Ceylon and started work on a tea plantation. He moved to Borneo, then settled in Malaya, where he became fascinated with local religious and magical beliefs. Until 1936 Gardner worked as a civil servant for the British, first as a rubber plantation inspector, then as a customs officer and inspector of opium houses. As an amateur archaeologist he made a name for himself in academic circles with his research into Malaya's early civilisation, and particularly their ritual knives and daggers. After 20 years of study he became the world's leading authority on Malaya's indigenous people and their weapons.

Back in England he became deeply fascinated with witchcraft, practising ritual and writing books. A contemporary described him as a 'vain, self-centred man, tight with his money and more interested in outlets for his nudist and voyeuristic activities than in learning anything about authentic witchcraft'.

Nonetheless, Gardner became a media celebrity, dubbed 'Britain's Chief Witch'; now Gardnerian Wicca is established as a leading tradition in witchcraft, held to be a remnant of an organised pagan religion that existed in Britain before the Puritan witch hunts.

asia & pacific rim

By the 1860s, trade and political relations between Britain and China had thrived to an extent that China decided to establish an embassy in England: the Chinese government appointed the American, Mr Anson Burlingham, who in 1861 had been American ambassador to China. The officials of the new Chinese Embassy arrived from New York on the Cunard steamship *Java*, which arrived in the Mersey flying the Chinese flag. Also in the ambassadorial party were two Chinese advisers, two secretaries (one Irish, one French), six Chinese interpreters, who spoke English, French and Russian, two Chinese writers, a Chinese doctor and 17 servants. All the Europeans had adopted Chinese names, and all wore Chinese dress. A Mr Earle, courier to the Embassy, had made reservations to stay at the Adelphi Hotel in Liverpool, before the party continued on to London. The procession, from the ship up to the hotel in Lime Street, of dignitaries, servants and vast amounts of baggage, caused quite a stir in the city, according to reports in the local paper. But to the huge embarrassment of all concerned, there were 'misunderstandings' (as the newspaper chose to put it) at the Adelphi over the party's suitability as guests, so the Chinese Emperor's American-born Ambassador and his cosmopolitan entourage were forced to stay at the Washington Hotel instead.

The first recorded incidence of racial prejudice against the Chinese in Liverpool.

ever told, so their ships had Homeric names) had a speed of 10 knots, single screw steam engines and were barque-rigged to make full use of the winds around the Cape of Good Hope.

At first the 12,530-mile homeward run from China took 58 days, but once the Suez Canal opened in 1869 the time was cut by up to 12 days.

Suez cut 3,000 miles off the east-west journey, but high towing charges and difficult winds in the Red Sea meant that the canal was suitable only for steam-ships; sailing ships still had to round the Cape of Good Hope.

The Holts were unique in being the only shipping line owners to be directly involved in the design and construction of their ships; Alfred Holt invented a new engine which used less coal and was more reliable, making voyages faster and more profitable. His marine engineering brilliance established his vessels as the worldwide benchmark of 'Holt Class' – which was not only for the quality of the ships, but of their crews, management and shore staff.

The world's first regular long-distance cargo liner service, the Blue Funnel's core business was to China and the Far East right up to the 1970s, although from the 1890s routes to America and Australia were added. In 1910, Blue Funnel started a passenger service to Australia via South Africa, using ships with refrigeration to bring back perishable goods such as fruit and meat.

Blue Funnel, known in Liverpool as the China Company, was one of the most important factors in establishing the city's Chinese community, employing many Chinese crew throughout the company's history: it was from the 1860s that the Chinese population really started to grow.

According to the official census, the number of Chinese in Liverpool and Birkenhead was 15 in 1881, 27 in 1891, and 76 in 1901; but these numbers are misleading since many Chinese, educated in China but illiterate in English, would not have completed the census.

The community settled around the south docks, especially around Pitt Street, Cleveland Square and York Street, where there were Chinese boarding houses, restaurants, grocery shops, clubs, houses and laundries.

Although most Chinese who came to Liverpool were merchant seamen rather than passengers, there were some who paid their passage here. In one case the captain of a ship took fares from several Chinese migrants, but once the ship sailed they were forced to work on board. When the ship docked in Liverpool, these men went ashore and they were classed as deserters. A few Chinese docked at other British ports and came to Liverpool by train to join the community.

Despite the peaceful success of the multicultural community in Liverpool, a journalist called Claude Blake wrote a sensa-

As there were few Chinese women in Liverpool, the men married local girls; British-born women lost their British citizenship when they married a Chinese man

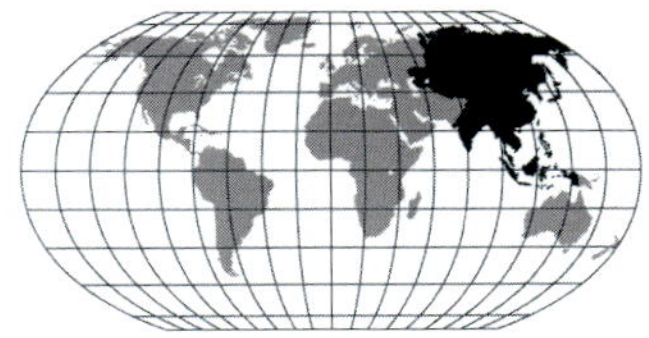

tional article in the Sunday Chronicle of 2 December 1906, accusing the British Chinese of vice and immorality. Liverpool city council set up a commission to investigate and found that not only could the Chronicle's allegations not be substantiated but, on the contrary, 'it is noteworthy that from the earliest years of their settlement, the Chinese have been regarded as the embodiment of public order'.

That year the Chinese Seamen's Union had been set up, as had the Chinese Progress Club in Pitt Street and the Chinese Masonic Club – a branch of the fraternal society known as All Men and Brothers – opened in Cleveland Square.

In both World Wars, many Chinese seamen served on board British ships, and one report stated: 'The heroism of Chinese sailors is beyond praise, and a number have been decorated by the King for gallantry.'

During World War 2 Liverpool was the home of the Chinese Merchant Seamen's Pool; there may have been as many as 20,000 Chinese men registered – most of whom came from the Chinese mainland, especially Shanghai – who were escaping political turmoil in China. Then, in the early 1940s, the Japanese occupied the Chinese treaty ports so that many Chinese men in Liverpool couldn't return home and were forced to stay here.

The decision to settle here meant, for most, marrying and having a family; as there were few Chinese women in Liverpool, the men tended to marry local girls – British-born women automatically lost their British citizenship when they married a Chinese man. For white women, Chinese men were preferable to local men because they were kinder, more

Night lights: Hong Kong harbour

asia & pacific rim

considerate and gentle. In many poor white households, the men would get drunk and beat the women and children – the Chinese were horrified by such behaviour, and by contrast would often, if they saw a child barefoot in the street, go and buy them shoes.

Within the Chinese community, there was little racial or religious strife between the various nationalities and cultures living in the area; the local school was nicknamed the League of Nations. There was only one recorded clash between Chinese and English men in Liverpool, reported in the local paper in 1910. But the Chinese Liverpudlians came up against discrimination when they tried to get jobs in the city; they still do.

The English perception that the Chinese were stupid or illiterate was far from the truth – they may have had little knowledge of the English language and English ways, but they were educated; in China more respect is given to intellectuals than to the wealthy. But, despite a higher level of educational qualifications than their English counterparts, a highly developed work ethic and entrepreneurial culture, Liverpool's Chinese still struggle to get decent jobs outside their own community.

At the start of the 1990s, there was a concerted campaign in Liverpool to draw on historical trading links with Shanghai, and in 1999 the twinning ceremony between Liverpool and Shanghai cemented the two cities' relationship. As a most generous gift to celebrate the connection, the city of Shanghai gave Liverpool an archway – the biggest outside mainland China. A team of civil engineers and skilled workmen came over to Liverpool to put the hundreds of pieces of this

Life on the water: Vietnam's Mekong river

In 1875 70,000 rubber tree seeds were sent from Brazil to Liverpool; two decades later the first rubber plantation was established in Malaya

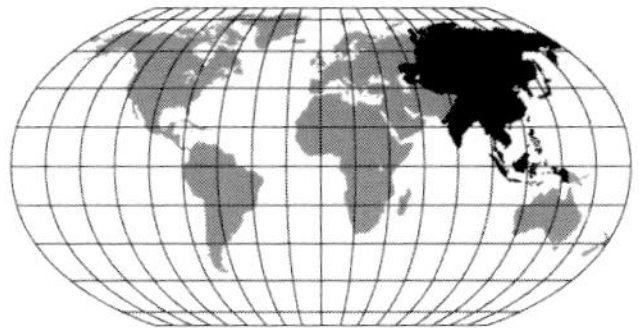

splendid, spectacular structure in place – it took several months, and was officially opened in September 2000. If there was ever any doubt where Chinatown was in Liverpool, there can be no doubt now.

With the arrival of new Chinese settlers – this time after the return of Hong Kong from British rule – Liverpool has another chance to make the most of an under-valued community that has contributed a good deal, taken very little and remained loyal to the city.

Maritime trade brought other Asians to Britain; lascar seamen – mostly Muslims from India, the Middle East and Africa – worked on East India Company ships, but after 1830 began to sign on with Liverpool ships. Indian lascars were recruited from Gujarat, Sind, Assam and Bengal and at the end of the 19th century represented 20% of the British maritime labour force.

Crews were recruited through kin networks by labour agents known as ghaut serangs; most men came from poor rural districts and went to sea as the best way of earning money for their families. A few of these crewmen would have settled in Liverpool, but the first significant groups from India to settle in Liverpool arrived in the early 1900s, most coming from the Punjab in north western India. Liverpool then had a reputation as a rich city, and people saw it as their route to a better life. They made their way to ports such as Karachi, Bombay and Calcutta – to find a place on ships bound for Liverpool. The journey could take up to three months, which for men with no experience of sea travel must have been daunting – and they arrived not speaking much English, with little money and nowhere to go. They had to take what work was available, and had to face hostility and discrimination when finding jobs and accommodation.

Some became street pedlars or entertainers, preferring to be self-employed than work for others.

Bahadur Singh came to Liverpool from Lahore (now in Pakistan) in 1929, aged 36. He worked as a fortune teller and a pedlar, selling clothes, toys, tools, kitchen utensils – whatever was in demand.

His wife Teka Devi eventually came to join him in Liverpool – one of the first Sikh women here and an important figure in the growing Indian community. Known as Maji (Mother) to many Indian immigrants in the 1940s and 1950s, she helped them find work, gave them a home and fed them, regardless of their religion.

Rasool Khan was a gifted magician and entertainer, known as the Gilly Gilly Man. He came to England in 1926 and lived in Sheffield for some years before bringing his family to Liverpool. He started his stage career in working men's clubs around the city before touring Europe and appearing on television as 'Rasool Hamza, Pakistan's Great Illusionist'.

The story of the rubber trade has several Liverpool connections. Once Thomas Hancock patented his vulcanisation process in 1843, manufacturers began producing rubber boots and shoes. The Liverpool Rubber Company began manufacturing under licence from Hancock in 1859; the factory in Rice Lane, Walton, began making galoshes, then men's rubber knee and thigh boots. Plimsolls began in 1868 and other designs followed. Supplies of rubber from the Amazon could not meet demand; so in 1875 Sir Joseph Hooker, director of the Royal Botanical Gardens at Kew, commissioned explorer HA Wickham to collect 70,000 rubber tree seeds; these were sent by chartered ship to Liverpool, and on to Kew. Nearly 2,000 seedlings were sent to Ceylon, and two decades later the first rubber plantation was established in Malaya, 'grandchildren' of the Brazilian seeds that were imported through Liverpool. Malaya quickly became the world's principal source of rubber.

By the end of the 19th century, half of all rubber imports were coming through the port of Liverpool.

In 1925 Dunlop bought the Liverpool Rubber Co and by 1930 production was up to four million pairs; rubber tyres were also made at the Speke factory. Dunlop acquired substantial rubber plantations in Malaya and Ceylon, and cotton mills in Lancashire, so Liverpool was a natural site for its factories. Dunlop closed both plants in the early 1970s, with 3,500 job losses.

africa & middle east

Liverpool's black population is as diverse as its white European population, with people coming here from all over Africa as well as America and the West Indies. But, of course, black Americans and Afro-Caribbeans trace their roots back to Africa and Liverpool, notoriously, played a major part in creating the black population of the Americas through the 18th century slave trade.

Liverpool has one of the oldest black populations in the UK, the early settlers mostly seamen recruited from West Africa, America or the West Indies. Some are descendants of African traders sent to Liverpool to be educated. There were also freed slaves (as soon as a slave set foot in England after 1772 he was a free man) and servants of wealthy families with slave connections.

Some freed slaves signed up as seamen on ships in the American Civil War and ended up in Liverpool that way.

A number of black Americans would have been among the thousands that came through Liverpool en route to France in the First World War – they were billeted at a vast camp in Knotty Ash – and huge numbers of army, navy and air force personnel were either stationed here or en route to other bases or front lines in Europe. Inevitably, some stayed here, married local women and had a family.

Liverpool's large Muslim community represents over 40 countries in Asia, Europe, America and Africa; global politics since the watershed of 9/11 have put the Muslim community in the spotlight and, in 2004, Liverpool's Year of Faith, there have been great efforts made by all faith communities to demonstrate that Muslims are peace-loving people. One of the Yemeni community's leaders said: 'We in Liverpool don't hold a grudge against anybody and we disapprove of all atrocities of fanatics.'

Liverpool's Al Rahma Mosque in Toxteth was built in 1974, after a ten-year wait for the city council's planning department to give the green light. More than 1,000 Muslims worship here every Friday and the community is talking about the need for a second mosque to cope with growing numbers.

Three distinct African communities – Yemeni, Somali and Nigerian – have grown up in Liverpool over many decades.

The Yemeni community is one of Liverpool's largest ethnic groups, but also one of its least known. After the Suez Canal opened in 1869, Yemenis who went to Aden – a British Protectorate – could get a British passport easily enough and took ship for Britain, where they established communities in the deep sea ports – Cardiff, London, Tyneside and Liverpool.

Now the city's Yemenis are raising their profile, setting up a national academic conference for Arabic arts and running an annual festival of Arabic culture.

The Somalis number about 4,000, mostly living in the Granby area of Toxteth. The first generation of Somali settlers were sailors working for the British Navy when the country, in the Horn of Africa, was British Somaliland.

Then a wave of Somalis came to Liverpool in the early 1990s, after war broke out in famine-hit Somalia in 1991; around 50,000 people were killed and another 300,000 died of starvation. Some of the refugees in Liverpool witnessed killings and destruction, loss and displacement; some are permanently disabled as a result of war injuries.

A nomadic people, the Somalis are very independent and protective of their cultural identity. Reluctant to integrate for fear of losing their identity, many Somali families have felt very isolated in Liverpool; this has meant a lot of misunderstanding about Somali culture.

The level of educational achievement for young Liverpudlian Somalis has, till now, been relatively low, as has their self-confidence, and unemployment levels are high. The community is eager to see a Somali academy linked to the universities, to help the young achieve their ambitions and make stronger links within the city.

The Nigerians first came to Liverpool when Nigeria was a British Protectorate (1914–60), as crew on Liverpool ships; many have since come here to study at

Reluctant to integrate for fear of losing their identity, many Somali families have felt very isolated in Liverpool

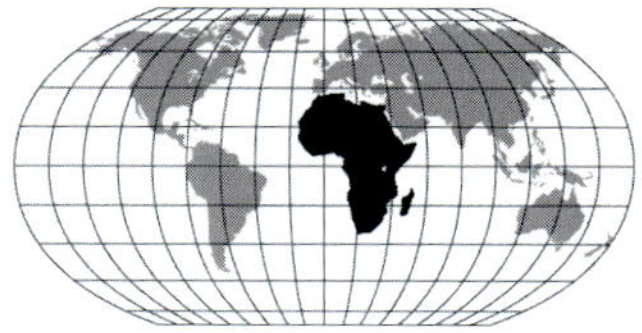

university and to start their careers. Angus Chukwemeka, chair of the Nigerian Community Association, came to Liverpool in 1968 to study electrical engineering; of his five children, one son is a barrister, one a pharmacist, and his daughter has just qualified in law.

But again, subtly racist attitudes have made it difficult for West Africans to prosper in the city. Despite being better qualified than many white Liverpudlians, Nigerians, like the Chinese, suffer far higher unemployment levels.

There may not be overt racist hostility, but one Nigerian businessman, who is a JP and has his own main contracting construction company, says: 'I have five A levels and two degrees, but it's impossible to open a bank account here as a black businessman.'

All is politeness and consideration, but the answer is still no. And the number of black senior managers or professionals is still negligible. For a city with such a cosmopolitan history, it is way beyond time to readjust the racist attitudes that waste talent and ambition on such a grand scale.

William Quilliam, a Liverpool lawyer, became a Muslim in 1887 after spending time in Algiers and Morocco.
Taking the name Sheikh Abdullah Quilliam, he became famous in the Muslim world as the author of *The Faith of Islam*, the first book in English by a Muslim. Quilliam also founded and edited The Crescent, a weekly national journal for Muslim intellectuals, from 1893 to 1908. He helped set up the Islamic Institute and opened Britain's first mosque, in 1889, at Brougham Terrace.

World Heritage Site at Giza, Egypt

africa & middle east

There is no evidence of a ship docking in Liverpool with a cargo of slaves, but some slaves were sold here. In 1758 Williamson's Advertiser announced: 'A beautiful negro boy for sale, well-proportioned, mild, sober and of honest disposition.' And another: 'A healthy negro girl aged about 15 years, speaks good English, works at her needle, washes well, does housework, and has had the small pox.'

Although there were some fabulously profitable voyages made by slavers, the average profit on a slave cargo was less than 10%, and some slavers made a loss. The key to making money, then, was volume. In 1702 alone, some 40,000 slaves were packed like sardines into the holds of Liverpool ships for sale in the Americas.

There is a myth that the Goree Warehouses (demolished after the Second World War) had iron rings to which slaves were chained. Not true – the Goree Warehouses (named after the slaving island of Gorée off West Africa) were not built until 1793; 21 years earlier, in 1772, a slave became free as soon as he set foot on English soil.

Nor are the chained figures on the Nelson Memorial African slaves. They represent four of Nelson's most famous victories during the Napoleonic Wars.

Liverpool came late to the slave trade – which was respectable in Elizabeth I's court. Slavery had, of course, been going on for centuries in Europe, the Middle East, Africa and Asia, and in some parts of the world it continues today.

Slave ships from England first carried white slaves – convicts, beggars and the unlucky – caught, transported and sold in America for tobacco, before merchants saw the potential of Africa.

Bristol and London had dominated the European trade of 'black gold' long before the *Liverpool Merchant* reached Barbados in 1700 with its cargo of 220 African slaves for sale. For the next 40 years Liverpool ships did not join the trade in any number, but for 60 years, to the turn of the 19th century, Liverpool was the leading slavery port, sending between 40 and 100 ships yearly on the infamous triangular journey, and accounting for up to half the world's trade in slaves from West Africa to America.

In 1771 alone Liverpool's 105 slave ships carried more slaves than the entire population of Liverpool. By the turn of the century, a quarter of Liverpool's ships were engaged in the slave trade – a tenth of Liverpool outbound shipping tonnage went to Africa carrying textiles, guns, iron, alcohol and beads.

These goods would be exchanged for men, women and children who might have been debtors or convicts, prisoners of war, or sold by relatives or elders.

Of the two million slaves taken from West Africa, fewer than 750,000 survived until 1825, either dying on the long journey, or from brutality and disease on the other side of the Atlantic. Slaves were packed like rows of books on shelves or herrings in a barrel, each with a space no more than 18 inches wide – less room than in a coffin; they were chained to each other hand and foot for up to 14 weeks, the period it took to cross the ocean.

Brutality and violence from and between crewmen was the order of the day. Ships' captains had an incentive to keep slaves alive and saleable, but they were mostly barbarous men. One captain, irritated by an African woman's anxiety for her sick child, snatched the baby from her, smashed its head against the side of the ship and threw it overboard.

In Liverpool an industry grew up making slavers' instruments: branding irons, handcuffs and shackles and the speculum oris, used to prise open a slave's mouth for force-feeding.

There were certainly some African slaves in Liverpool. In Bold Street high-class whores paraded slave boys in gold and silver collars, and black child slaves were the height of fashion for wealthy society ladies.

The rights and wrongs of the slave trade caused bitter controversy. In a famous incident at a Liverpool theatre, actor George Cooke was provoked into yelling

A quarter of Liverpool's ships were engaged in the slave trade – a tenth of Liverpool outbound shipping tonnage went to Africa

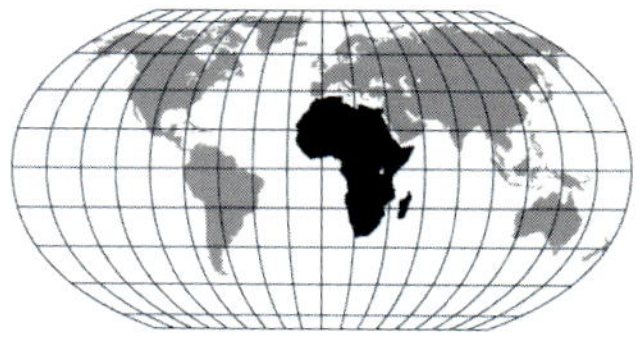

at his audience: 'I have not come here to be insulted by a set of wretches, every brick in whose infernal town is cemented with an African's blood.'

Men like William Rathbone, Dr Binns and William Roscoe campaigned, against ferocious opposition, for the abolition of slavery, founding the Society for Abolition in 1787. Although initially blocked by the House of Lords, the Act abolishing the trade in slaves was passed in 1807, no thanks to 64 petitions from Liverpool slavers to Parliament.

In July 1807 the *Kitty's Amelia*, under Captain Hugh Crow, became the last Liverpool ship to leave the Mersey to buy 'black ivory' to take across the Atlantic.

Sculptural evidence of African trade can be seen at the Town Hall – where there are stone carvings of African people, lions, elephants and crocodiles. Next door, in Water Street, is Barclays Bank – formerly the Martins Bank building. In the doorway are stone friezes depicting two African children carrying bags, symbolising the wealth of Africa.

In August 2001 Liverpool enacted a ceremony of cleansing and forgiveness – Duae – performed by African chiefs, after the city of Liverpool made formal apologies for its part in the slave trade. The ceremony was part of the International Day for Remembrance of Slavery and its Abolition, organised by Liverpool both to acknowledge the shameful past and to celebrate the city's multicultural inheritance. Duae (an Ashanti word meaning pardon) included an Act of Libation at Canning Dock, which called on the souls of past, present and future generations to witness this cleansing act of forgiveness.

The African elephant in the South African bush

Village life: Siovonga, Zimbabwe

africa & middle east

In 1756, Olaudah Equiano was 11 years old. Captured and sold into slavery, he was flung into an extraordinary life that ended in Britain. Educated and free, Equiano wrote his autobiography when he was 44: *The Interesting Narrative of the Life of Olaudah Equiano, or Gustavus Vassa, the African.*

Born into a wealthy Ibo family of judges in the kingdom of Benin, on the Niger River, Equiano had a happy childhood and a secure future. Slavery was an integral part of many African peoples; Equiano's family owned slaves. But when Equiano was captured he was to suffer the horrific cruelty of the triangular trade. After six months with a series of African masters, he was sold to English slave traders and shipped to Barbados. From there he was sent to Virginia and sold to a Royal Navy lieutenant, Michael Henry Pascal. Equiano was Pascal's slave for seven years, in which time he travelled the world on ships under Pascal's command.

He also educated himself, while in England, and in 1766, aged 21, he bought his freedom and went into trade in the West Indies, and then in London.

In 1773, Equiano was a member of an expedition – unsuccessful – to discover the fabled Northwest Passage, a sea route from the Atlantic, through the Arctic Ocean to the Pacific.

In England, Equiano became a fervent abolitionist, travelling the country lecturing against the slave trade and working to resettle freed slaves. The bloody trade, which created so much wealth for Liverpool, was abolished ten years after Equiano's death in 1797.

The following extract from Equiano's autobiography gives a rare literary insight into the long nightmare that was known as the Middle Passage: the side of the shipping triangle, between Africa and the West Indies, that carried human cargo.

Pause for thought: Siovonga, Zimbabwe

I even wished for my former slavery in preference to my present situation, which was filled with horrors of every kind

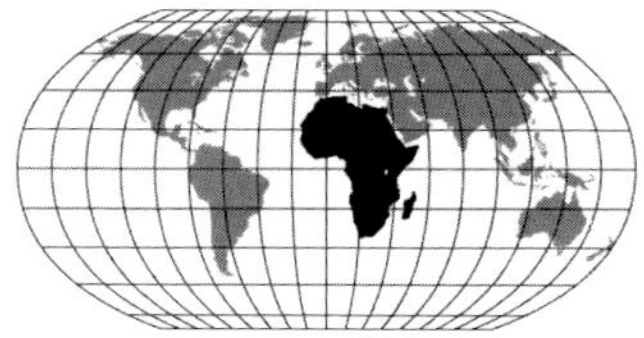

'I continued to travel, sometimes by land, sometimes by water, through different countries and various nations, till, at the end of six or seven months after I had been kidnapped, I arrived at the sea coast. The first object which saluted my eyes when I arrived on the coast was the sea, and a slave ship, which was waiting for its cargo. These filled me with astonishment, which was converted into terror, when I was carried on board. I was handled to see if I were sound, by some of the crew; and I was now persuaded that I had gotten into a world of bad spirits, and that they were going to kill me.

'I now saw myself deprived of all chance of returning to my native country, or even the least glimpse of hope of gaining the shore, which I now considered friendly; and I even wished for my former slavery in preference to my present situation, which was filled with horrors of every kind, still heightened by my ignorance of what I was to undergo.

'I was soon put down under the decks, and there I received such a salutation in my nostrils as I had never experienced in my life: so that, with the loathsomeness of the stench, and crying together, I became so sick and low that I was not able to eat, nor had I the least desire to taste anything. I now wished for the last friend, death, to relieve me; but soon, two of the white men offered me eatables; and, on my refusing to eat, one of them held me fast by the hands, and laid me across, I think, the windlass, and tied my feet, while the other flogged me severely.

'The white people looked and acted, as I thought, in so savage a manner; for I had never seen among any people such instances of brutal cruelty; and this not only shown towards us blacks, but also to some of the whites themselves. One white man I saw flogged so unmercifully with a large rope, that he died in consequence of it; and they tossed him over the side as they would have done a brute.

'The closeness of the place, and the heat of the climate, added to the number in the ship, which was so crowded that each had scarcely room to turn himself, almost suffocated us. This produced copious perspirations, so that the air soon became unfit for respiration, from a variety of loathsome smells, and brought on a sickness among the slaves, of which many died – falling victims to the improvident avarice, as I may call it, of their buyers.

'This wretched situation was again aggravated by the gaffing of the chains, and the filth of the necessary tubs, into which the children often fell and were almost suffocated. The shrieks of the women, and the groans of the dying, rendered the whole a scene of horror almost inconceivable.

'At last we came in sight of the island of Barbadoes, at which the whites on board gave a great shout. As the vessel drew nearer, we saw the harbor, and other ships of different kinds and sizes, and we soon anchored amongst them, off Bridgetown. Many merchants and planters now came on board; they put us in separate parcels, and examined us attentively. They also made us jump, and pointed to the land, signifying we were to go there. We thought by this, we should be eaten by these ugly men, as they appeared to us; and there was nothing but bitter cries to be heard all the night.

'We were conducted to the merchant's yard, where we were all pent up together, like so many sheep in a fold, without regard to sex or age. On a signal given, the buyers rush at once into the yard where the slaves are confined, and make choice of that parcel they like best.

'I remember, in the vessel in which I was brought over, there were several brothers, who were sold in different lots; and it was very moving on this occasion, to see and hear their cries at parting.

'O, ye nominal Christians! might not an African ask you – learned you this from your God, Do unto all men as you would men should do unto you? Is it not enough that we are torn from our country and friends, to toil for your luxury and lust of gain? Must every tender feeling be sacrificed to your avarice? Why are parents to lose their children, brothers their sisters, or husbands their wives? Surely, this is a new refinement in cruelty, which, while it has no advantage to atone for it, thus aggravates distress, and adds fresh horrors even to the wretchedness of slavery.'

africa & middle east

The big yellow statue on Liverpool's dock road – Super Lamb Banana – is a reference to the fact that the first bananas imported to Britain came through Liverpool in 1884. It was Alfred Lewis Jones, then a partner in the shipping line Elder Dempster, who encouraged the British to eat bananas for their health-giving properties, and Elder Dempster's association with the African fruit trade got them dubbed the banana boats. Alfred Jones was born in Wales in 1845, and came to Liverpool, aged 12, as an apprentice to the managers of the African Steamship Company, making several voyages to West Africa. By the age of 26 he was manager of the business, but after a few years set up his own successful shipping company. In 1897 John Dempster and Alexander Elder, who had bought the African Steamship Company, offered Jones a directorship and by 1890 Jones had a controlling interest. Knighted in 1901, Sir Alfred Lewis Jones was heavily involved in opening up and developing West Africa, and at the start of the 20th century took the lead in opening up the West Indies and stimulating Jamaica's fruit trade as well as tourist traffic. A powerful philanthropist, Jones founded the world's first School of Tropical Medicine in Liverpool – still the leading organisation of its kind. The School's first Nobel Prize came to Sir Ronald Ross in 1902 for his discovery that malaria is transmitted by the bite of the anophiles mosquito.

Sir Alfred Lewis Jones died in 1909.

There is, of course, more to African trade than slavery; Liverpool merchants have been doing legitimate business with African merchants for several hundred years, even in the 18th century, when the fattest profits were made from buying and selling human beings.

Main imports from West Africa, for instance, were palm oil, cocoa, timber and ground nuts. Palm oil, not particularly glamorous, was nevertheless a vital commodity for industrial England. Its use grew rapidly in the 19th century, so that by 1815 some 52% of Liverpool's imports from West Africa was palm oil; by 1830 Liverpool was importing 96% of all palm oil imported into Britain.

The oil was used to lubricate industrial machinery, to moisturise wool in the mills, to make soap (for washing cotton in Lancashire mills) and to make candles (Merseyside was then the candle-making centre of England).

Today it is not just commodities imported from Africa and the Middle East, but the culture itself: two shops in Liverpool offer a taste of the Muslim world.

The Olive Tree in Renshaw Street stocks books about Islam, but the shop is also crammed with colourful objects – rugs, cushions, hand-embroidered fabrics, clothes, ceramics, glass – from Egypt, Syria, the Gulf, Morocco and many other countries, as well as local Muslim crafts and calligraphy. The shop's name refers to the olive tree growing in countries that lie between the east and the west, as a peaceful symbol of Islam bringing the world together.

In Smithdown Road, Sam Naji has opened her shop, Mystical, selling Arab, African and Asian clothes and jewellery, perfumes and incense. Born to Yemeni parents in California, Sam married a family friend in the Yemen when she was 13 and lived there for three years before moving to Liverpool, where her husband had lived since he was a child.

Marriage is also what turned Joao Roberto into a confirmed Scouser. Born in the Cape Verde Islands, 280 miles off the west coast of Africa, near Senegal, Joao joined the British Merchant Navy; when his ship berthed at Liverpool, Joao went ashore, met and fell in love with a local girl, and stayed. He worked as a waiter before opening his own Portuguese restaurant, the Algarve, in Stanley Street.

In 2002, Joao Roberto became Britain's first honorary consul for the Republic of Cape Verde. 'One of the main purposes is to help seafarers who come to Liverpool,' he explained, 'but I also want to create some kind of cultural exchange between the islands and the UK, especially with Liverpool.'

The islands were colonised by the Portuguese in the 15th century and were a centre for the Portuguese slave trade; Cape Verde, with a population of 405,000 (about the same as Liverpool) won its independence in 1975.

Super Lamb Banana is a reference to the fact that the first bananas imported to Britain came through Liverpool, from Africa, in 1884

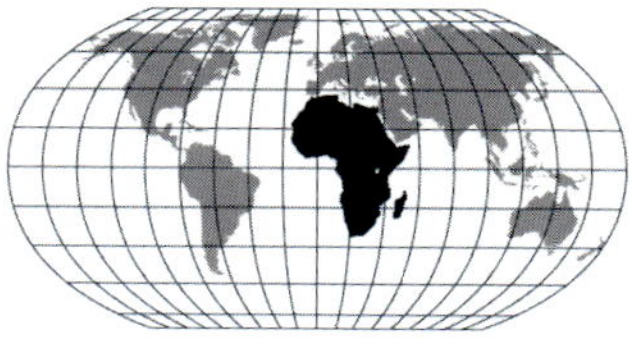

Giraffe, overshadowed by Mount Kilimanjaro, Kenya

the americas

It sounds like a pub quiz question: where are Liverpool FC and Everton FC separated by 1,000 miles? The answer is South America: to the east, Uruguay, where Liverpool Futbol Club in Montevideo plays in the premier division; to the west, Chile, where you can find CD Everton in the resort of Viña del Mar.

In 1908, a school side in Uruguay's capital city had to decide on a team name; they looked at a map during a geography lesson and picked Liverpool, a name that meant wealth and power.

The following year, after Everton FC had had a successful tour of South America, a group of footie fans in Valparaiso agreed that Everton would be a good name for their own team. So Corporacion Deportiva Everton was born. Now based in Viña del Mar, a few miles from the capital Valparaiso, CD Everton has its stadium on the edge of Lake Sausalito; the club's fans in Chile and in Liverpool are known as Ruleteros, or men who gamble on the spinning of a wheel.

Montevideo and Valparaiso, of course, are major South American ports with long trading links to Liverpool. Liverpool ship owners Lamport & Holt ran regular mail services to Brazil and the River Plate; up to 1851 the sailing ships took between 60 to 90 days; once steamships came in the average journey time dropped to 34 days from Liverpool to Buenos Aires, via Brazil and Uruguay.

On 15 June 1868, WJ Lamport wrote to a client: 'The number of British settlers in [Argentina and Uruguay] is immensely large – and unlike most other fields which attract immigration, they comprise all classes of society from the upper middle-class downwards. A very great number of the estancias [ranches] and saladeros [meat-salting plants] in the country are the property of and managed and worked by Englishmen.'

Argentina was a key destination for people leaving Liverpool – half the total number of migrants travelling to Argentina from around the world embarked from Mersey docks.

Liverpool merchants began trading with South America as early as 1666, when the *Antelope* set off for Barbados and brought

Icebergs in Glacier Lake
Torres del Paine, Chile

It was strongly rumoured that the Guyanese Nondescript bore a startling resemblance to Mr Lushington, the Liverpool customs inspector

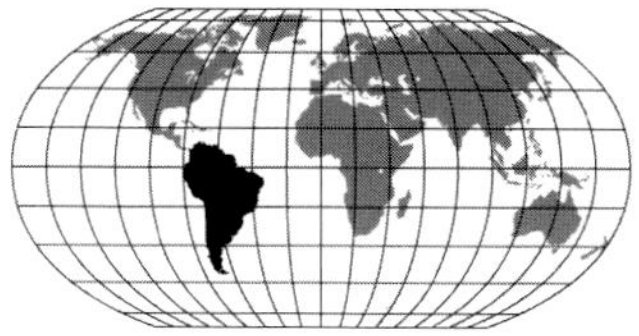

back a cargo of sugar cane. It wasn't long before sugar refiners started to set up in Liverpool; the first two sugar entrepreneurs were Allyn Smith, a notable sugar baker from London, and partners Richard Cleveland and Daniel Danvers. Both houses were built in the 1670s. Smith, according to Sir Edward Moore who sold him the land, was expecting at least £40,000 of trade per year from Barbados.

In 1704 only 760 tons of raw sugar was imported through Liverpool, but by 1785 this had risen to 16,600 tons, supplying a dozen sugar houses in the town. Sugar arrived from Barbados and Demerara as a dark sticky molasses; treacle, syrup, sugar loaves and granulated sugar were all stages in the evolution of the refining process.

Liverpool merchants and planters in Liverpool formed the West Indies Association in 1799, to look after the interests of their trade, including a check on Customs & Excise duties.

One of the great innovators and entrepreneurs of the sugar industry was Henry Tate. Now a household name, Tate in 1859 was a grocer, when he joined the sugar refinery of John Wright & Co in Manesty Lane. Tate then started his own refinery in 1862 in Earle Street; swift expansion and a move to Love Lane saw Tate's output rise to 20,000 tons a year.

In 1924 Tate's merged with Lyle's of Greenock, and the famous brand name was born. The Love Lane refinery reached a production peak in its centenary year, 1972, with 550,000 tons of sugar leaving the factory gates.

Tate & Lyle closed the Love Lane plant in 1981, a major blow to the people of Vauxhall. The opening in 1988 of the northern branch of the Tate Gallery in Liverpool was a gesture, but not exactly a replacement for the lost jobs.

Trade broadened in the early 1800s, taking coal and mail out to Brazil, Argentina and the west coast, and bringing back cargoes of coffee, copper ore and nitrates – in the form of guano (bird droppings) for use as fertiliser.

In the second half of the 19th century, shippers began to import grain, refrigerated meat and other foods to cater for the fast-growing towns of northern England.

The danger in maritime trade with South America was that in reaching the west coast – Chile, Peru, Ecuador, Colombia, and north to America's western seaboard – ships had to round Cape Horn. Treacherous currents, storms and dangerous winds have wrecked countless ships. One that survived 22 years of sailing was the *Jhelum.* Built in Liverpool in 1849, the 428-ton sailing ship sailed regularly round the Horn for copper and guano; but in 1871 she was damaged and abandoned in Port Stanley in the Falkland Islands. She is beached there still, the world's only accessible example of a mid-19th century Liverpool-built sailing ship.

Cape Horn was a hazard for shipping until the Panama Canal opened in 1914.

On 28 May 1865, 153 Welsh men, women and children left Liverpool in a tea-clipper, bound for Patagonia, on the southernmost tip of South America. Three years later there were 5,000 of them there, and Welsh is still spoken in Patagonia.

When in 1821 eccentric English naturalist Charles Waterton brought back hundreds of specimens of wildlife from South America – all safely stuffed – his boat docked in Liverpool and he encountered a customs inspector called Lushington, who insisted that Waterton pay the highest import tax he could impose. Three years later, in the jungles of Guyana, Waterton 'discovered' an extraordinary creature he called the Nondescript, which he carefully preserved and brought back to England. Looking like a human head, except for a thick coat of fur around the exposed face, sceptical scientists said the thing was not real, but more likely a face moulded out of the hind quarters of a howler monkey. Not only that, but it was strongly rumoured that the Nondescript bore a startling resemblance to Mr Lushington, the Liverpool customs inspector. Waterton never said a word.

Sir Titus Salt, the industrialist who built the village of Saltaire near Bradford, made a fortune importing alpaca wool, shipped to Liverpool from South America, then transported along the Leeds-Liverpool Canal to Saltaire for weaving.

When you're going to San Fransisco: the Golden Gate Bridge
San Fransisco, California

the americas

Once the Pilgrim Fathers had sailed off across the Atlantic to found the colony of New England, there flowed a steady stream of migrants looking for religious freedom and better economic prospects.

One of Liverpool's first emigrants to America was one Richard Mather. Born in 1596, Mather was a Puritan preacher, the first minister of the Ancient Chapel of Toxteth, where he preached his first sermon in 1618.

Continually under fire for his Puritan nonconformity, Mather was suspended in 1633 for non-compliance and in 1634 for having never worn a surplice in his 15 years of ministry.

'Better for him that he had gotten seven bastards', as the Archbishop of York put it. Mather gave up on England and, in search of freedom in church government and the way he wanted to minister, he sailed to New England in June 1635, where he settled in Dorchester and became the leader of Congregationalism in Massachusetts. Incidentally, the portrait of Mather by John Foster is thought to be the first woodcut printed in America, in 1670.

Richard Mather's son, Increase, became president of Harvard, and Increase's son Cotton Mather was possibly the most famous of the family, first for his part in the Salem Witch Trials of 1692, then as President of Yale, then as the man who set up a school to educate slaves, and introduced inoculation to a smallpox-ridden Boston.

One of the most extraordinary stories that links Liverpool with America is that of Robert Morris, whose name should be as well known as that of Thomas Jefferson, George Washington or Benjamin Franklin. Morris's relative obscurity – certainly in his birthplace – is bizarre, given the scale of his achievements and his place in American history.

The man who financed the American Revolution, Robert Morris was one of only two people (with Roger Sherman) to sign the three key documents creating the American Republic – the Declaration of Independence, the Articles of Confederation, and the Constitution.

'Bold and enterprising, of great mercantile knowledge, fertile in expedients and an able financier. Very popular in and out of Congress .... grown extremely rich.' So said a contemporary of Morris, who had come a very long way from his origins in Liverpool.

Born in Chorley Court, off Dale Street, close to the Town Hall, on 20 January 1734, Robert Morris was the son of a man engaged in the tobacco trade, and in 1747 emigrated to join his father in Maryland. The family moved to Philadelphia the following year, but Morris's father was killed soon after in an accident. Robert, then 15, became apprenticed to the merchant Charles Willing, and by the age of 20 had become Thomas Willing's partner. The firm became New England's leading import-export house, and Morris's reputation grew rapidly.

In 1765 Morris served on a committee to protest against the Stamp Act; he believed that taxes imposed by the British Parliament without the consent of colonial governments equalled a form of taxation without representation, and an abuse of their ancient rights as English citizens.

After the Boston Tea Party and the imposition of the Coercive Acts by Britain, Morris was one of those to sign the Association's non-importation agreement in 1774, and in 1775 was elected to the Second Continental Congress. Now a committed revolutionary, Morris became warden of the port of Philadelphia in 1776 and showed considerable courage by staying in Philadelphia after the British captured the city.

Early in 1776, Morris was given a special commission by Congress, with authority to finance the operations of war. Later that year, George Washington wrote to Morris begging him to find $10,000 to shore up the desperate Continental Army. Morris arranged the loan himself to provision the troops at Valley Forge, who went on to win the Battle of Trenton and turn the course of the war.

Morris became chairman of the Finance Committee in 1778 and was on the Committee of Secret Correspondence, negotiating the alliance with France. By this time his influence was so strong that he, along with Richard Lee and the Adams brothers, could be said to have

Americans owe as much to the financial operations of Robert Morris as to the negotiations of Benjamin Franklin, or even the arms of George Washington

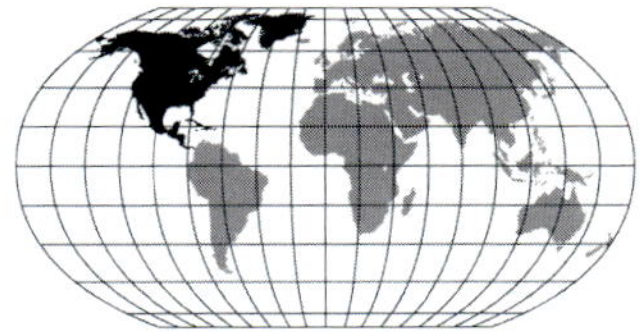

controlled Congress.

In 1779 the army was again desperately short of supplies, and again Washington wrote for help, this time to another Liverpool-born revolutionary, Judge Richard Peters, who came to Morris. Between them they bought 90 tons of lead and sent it to Washington.

As Superintendent of Finance from 1781 to 1784, Morris once again saved the country from financial ruin in the last years of the revolution, personally buying supplies for the forces and waging a crusade against waste and overspending, often risking everything by personally underwriting government debts.

Morris set up the Bank of North America with his own money, that of friends and colleagues, and French backers; it was Morris who nominated Washington to be President.

Washington then offered Morris the post of Secretary of Treasury in the new government, but he refused, and became one of Pennsylvania's first senators.

In an extraordinary twist of bitter irony, Morris's fortunes collapsed after speculative land deals in the District of Columbia and further west, and in 1798 he was thrown into a debtors' prison for four years.

He died in 1806, aged 73, his grand Philadelphia mansion unfinished, and his exemplary reputation as a financier, manager and administrator of the highest order, was in tatters.

As one historian put it: 'Certainly the Americans owed and still owe as much acknowledgement to the financial operations of Robert Morris as to the negotiations of Benjamin Franklin, or even the arms of George Washington.'

Fishing vessels in port at Corn Island
Nicaragua

the americas

Seven years after Independence, George Washington appointed James Maury as American Consul in Liverpool. Maury – who had been at school with future president Thomas Jefferson – sailed to Liverpool with fellow diplomats John Adams and John Jay, who then travelled to London and Paris respectively. It may only be by a matter of days, but Liverpool had the world's first American consulate.

James Maury lived in Liverpool for 40 years, from 1790 to 1829; his house was at 4 Rodney Street, and his office was in Paradise Street, by the Pool. Not all his consulate roles were glamorous – almost his first and last jobs were to bail out American sailors who had been chucked into the Tower of Liverpool for brawling or similar offences committed after getting pie-eyed in one of Liverpool's 2,300 pubs.

One of Maury's successors was Nathaniel Hawthorne, US Consul in Liverpool and author of books such as *The Scarlet Letter* and *Tanglewood Tales.* Hawthorne hated Liverpool: 'what with brutal ships' masters, drunken sailors, vagrant Yankees, mad people, sick people and dead people'. Not a sociable man: in four years 'I have received and been civil to at least 10,000 visitors ... and I never wish to be civil to anybody again.' Still, there were compensations. One of the consul's jobs was to certify invoices for exports: at $2 per autograph, and up to 25 invoices a day, it was significant extra income for the poor man.

Less than 100 years after fighting off British rule, the Americans then fought amongst themselves. The Civil War ran from 1861 to 1865, and Liverpool was at the start and finish of it. The first shot of the war was fired from a cannon made in

Sunset over Copacabana beach
Rio de Janeiro, Brazil

Waddell sailed to Liverpool, sure of a more lenient welcome than back in America, and surrendered *Shenandoah* to Liverpool's Mayor at the Town Hall

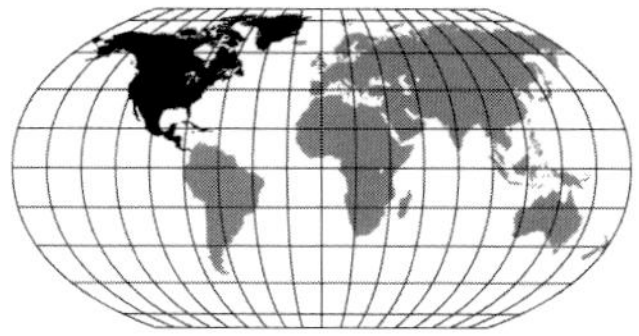

Duke Street by Fawcett & Preston ('Fosset' guns were used by both sides).

Confederate president Jefferson Davis sent a naval lieutenant, James Dunwoody Bulloch, to Liverpool with a brief to get arms and commission ships to break the Union blockade. Liverpool had, after all, strong commercial ties with the southern states. Bulloch signed contracts with local ship-builders for the first two commerce raiders – *Alabama* and *Florida* – in 1861; 35 blockade-runners were built on Merseyside for the Confederate cause. *CSS Florida* sank 36 ships; under Captain Raphael Semmes – with a largely Liverpudlian crew – *CSS Alabama* sank or captured 68 ships before being sunk by Federal cruiser *Kearsage* in the English Channel.

The *Alabama* was built by Lairds with a mix of sail and steam; she undertook sea trials with Bulloch and a small group of dignitaries on board. Only Bulloch and the captain Matthew Butcher knew that the ship was destined for the Confederate cause; the VIP party was put ashore at the Mersey Bar, and the ship sailed on to the Azores, where she was handed over to the command of Raphael Semmes.

The destruction caused by Mersey-built ships prompted the Federal government, after the war, to take Britain to the first international tribunal, in Geneva. The USA was awarded $15.5 million.

While fellow agent Isidor Straus was allowed to return home (he eventually bought Macy's department store in New York and became fabulously wealthy: he died on the *Titanic*), James Bulloch was exiled after the war. He became a cotton broker in Liverpool, where he was visited by his nephew Teddy Roosevelt. Bulloch died in 1898 and is buried in Toxteth cemetery; the Daughters of the Confederacy put up a tombstone in 1968.

In Abercromby Square, No 19 was built for CK Prioleau, a Confederate agent (whose wife was supposed to have been the most beautiful woman in Liverpool) working for Bulloch. Over the front door fanlight is the Bonnie Blue star of South Carolina; there are more on the entrance columns, while painted on the ceiling inside the door is the palmetto, the South Carolina state tree.

Foreign bankers to the Confederacy, Charleston cotton brokers Fraser Trenholm & Co had their offices at 10 Rumford Place.

The last act of the Civil War was played out in Liverpool, too. The Confederate ship *Shenandoah* had been raiding Union whaling ships in the Behring Strait. On 28 June her captain, Lt Cdr James Waddell, finally had news of Robert E Lee's surrender to Grant, and the end of the war. Waddell sailed to Liverpool, sure of a more lenient welcome than back in America, and surrendered *Shenandoah* to Liverpool's Mayor at the Town Hall on 6 November 1865, 211 days after the war ended. Waddell and his crew were arrested, but were then immediately liberated.

Richard Peters, born in Liverpool in 1704, was the son of Town Clerk Ralph Peters, and sailed to America in 1735. With Benjamin Franklin he founded the academy that would become the University of Philadelphia.
His nephew, also Richard Peters, was born in Philadelphia in 1744. Becoming a lawyer in 1763, he was made Register of the Admiralty in 1771. In June 1776 Congress elected him secretary of the Continental Board of War and he became a lifelong friend of George Washington. In 1791 Peters was speaker of the State Senate. He died in 1828.

Thomas Jefferson, author of the Constitution and America's third President, met Liverpool polymath William Roscoe while in Europe and they corresponded ever after. In a letter to Roscoe of 27 December 1820, Jefferson wrote: 'Your Liverpool [Royal] Institution will also aid us in the organisation of our new University [of Virginia].'

Banastre Tarleton, born in Water Street in 1754, was 22 when he went to America to fight for King George in the Revolution. He captured General Charles Lee from behind enemy lines and played a leading role in taking Philadelphia and Charleston, before being captured by Washington at York Town in 1781. He was a national hero in England, but his boast that he had laid more women and slaughtered more men than anyone else in the army earned him the nickname of The Butcher. He came home as a Major General.

Penguins at the South Pole

the americas

Emigrants, sailors and merchants took Liverpool with them to America:

Liverpool, Nova Scotia – On another Mersey River flowing into Liverpool Bay, this county town near Halifax was founded in 1759 and is known as the Port of Privateers.

Liverpool, Illinois – A riverside community with 136 residents; the first settlers arrived in 1826 and fishing was the main activity. At the turn of the 20th century hauls of 125,000 pounds of fish were recorded in a single day.

Liverpool, New York State – A suburb of Syracuse dating back to the 1850s. Salt and willow baskets were staple industries.

Liverpool Township, Ohio – The population is now 4,400; founded in 1816, it is now the Frog Jump capital of the USA. The first Frog Jump was held in 1962 and 7,500 people came to watch 132 frogs.

Liverpool, Pennsylvania – On the Susquehannah River in Perry County, with 934 Liverpoolite residents; it was founded in 1908.

Liverpool, Texas – This farming settlement in Brazoria County began as a trading post in 1827, founded by one Commodore Nelson; the population in 1990 was 396.

Below the statue of Christopher Columbus outside the Palm House in Sefton Park are the words: 'The discoverer of America was the maker of Liverpool.' Trade with America was so great that an American Chamber of Commerce was set up in Liverpool in 1801 and operated for 100 years. But it wasn't all one-way traffic.

Liverpool saw the arrival of some famous North American names, some of whom would make their fortune and become famous here.

A Quaker family from Shropshire called Cunard, for instance, sailed to Philadelphia in the 1600s, then moved to Halifax, Nova Scotia, where Samuel Cunard was born in 1787. The Cunard line was founded as the British & North American Royal Mail Steam Packet Company, when Samuel Cunard won the contract from the British Admiralty to carry the mail across the Atlantic. It was the beginning of a shipping legend, and although Cunard is now part of a Florida-based corporation, the Liverpool ties are still there; visits from the Cunard Queens (*QE2* and now *QM2*) draw huge crowds on the banks of the Mersey.

Many American writers braved the Atlantic to visit Liverpool. Mark Twain lectured at the Mechanics Institute; Harriet Beecher Stowe, famous for *Uncle Tom's Cabin*, was a visitor to Speke Hall.

Moby Dick author Herman Melville, trying to get into the Lyceum gentlemen's club in Bold Street, was thrown out by the seat of his pants. He used his memories of Liverpool in his book *Redburn*.

Washington Irving was in Liverpool for four years, managing his brother's business at 1 Goree Warehouses; when the business went bust, Irving had a breakdown and, during his convalescence, wrote *Rip Van Winkle* and *The Legend of Sleepy Hollow*.

In the 1820s James Audubon came to Liverpool with several hundred drawings; his exhibition at the Royal Institution in Colquitt Street was a great success and, with financial backing from the Rathbones, he published his four-volume *Birds of America*. Three of Audubon's oils are in the university's art gallery in Abercromby Square.

The patron of American painter James McNeill Whistler was the shipping magnate FR Leyland, who lived for some years at Speke Hall; Whistler was a frequent visitor after moving to England in 1859: at least, until he fell out with Leyland, owing him a lot of money. In the 1870s Whistler painted several portraits of Leyland (*Arrangement in Black*), his wife Frances (*Symphony in Flesh Colour and Pink*) and daughter Florence.

An entertaining visitor to Liverpool was Colonel William F Cody – Buffalo Bill – who brought his Wild West Show (with 400 performers including Little Annie Oakley, Sioux, Araphoe and Cheyenne Indians); in 1891 they performed in Newsham Park; 15 years later they were

Moby Dick author Herman Melville, trying to get into the Lyceum gentlemen's club in Bold Street, was thrown out by the seat of his pants

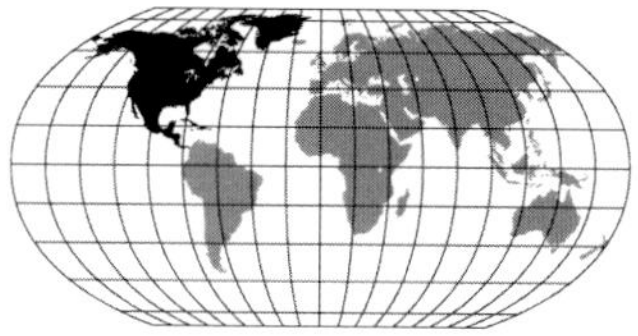

back with a show at the Exhibition Ground in Edge Lane.

Hollywood cowboy Roy Rogers and his wife Dale came to Liverpool in 1954 and stayed at the Adelphi Hotel. Roy rode his horse Trigger up the steps of the hotel, and later Trigger appeared at a first floor window to greet his fans.

Comedian and actor Mike Myers' (*Austin Powers, Wayne's World*) excellent Liverpool accent and Beatles fixation is down to his Scouse parents, who emigrated to Canada two years before Mike was born.

The two 20th century World Wars saw a massive influx of American armed forces into Liverpool. In World War 1 Liverpool's temporary home for US soldiers was the huge army camp at Knotty Ash; there was also an American military hospital at Mossley Hill.

America's entry into World War 2 came after November 1941, when the Japanese bombed Pearl Harbor; it wasn't long before troop ships were steaming across the Atlantic. Nearly 1,300 convoys, some of more than 60 ships, docked in Liverpool during the war (during the first half of 1944 alone some 750,000 men and two million tons of war supplies were unloaded at Liverpool). Ships would be queuing in the Mersey to dock, and troop trains were running incessantly from Riverside. With the huge US air base at Burtonwood, about 20 miles inland, USAF personnel, not to mention thousands of aircraft, were shipped through Liverpool.

In 1945, of course, the process was reversed, with hundreds of thousands of Americans going home, to be followed by 70,000 GI brides.

Storms made transatlantic trade hazardous, with ships being driven on to rocky coastlines, like this inlet in Nicaragua

the americas

From 1830 to 1930 Liverpool was the point of departure for nine million emigrants to America. By the mid-19th century there was an insatiable demand in America for labour; wages were about five times higher than in Europe, and almost 1,000 ships a year were taking emigrants from Liverpool.

It was no picnic: the crossing could take anything from a month to 14 weeks. Conditions on board depended on the price of the ticket. First class was relative luxury; second class at least provided a cabin. In steerage, where most people travelled, it was bunk beds sandwiched between the deck and the hold; a berth for four people could be as little as six feet square; it was cramped, badly lit, smelly and stuffy.

Food was poor and water was disgusting. Disease (including cholera), fire, ship-wreck and seasickness killed many; on one ship going to Quebec in 1847, 158 passengers died of typhus or cholera. Many ships were lost in storms, others were destroyed by fire; sometimes ships collided, many were wrecked on rocky coastlines. In 1854 a storm drove one ship on to rocks off the Irish coast, killing 370 out of 400 passengers and crew.

Even when they reached America there was no guarantee of a better life. In 1854 and 1855 unemployment in America was so bad that 30,000 immigrants were forced to sail back to Liverpool.

Of the 131,121 emigrants leaving Liverpool in 1848, 190 went to the West Indies, 298 to Australia, 14 to Hong Kong, 12 to the Falkland Islands and the rest to America and Canada. 1852 was the peak of emigration from Liverpool: 299,099

Malibu's curved coastline, California

The water jug is plunging and leaping like a lively dolphin. All the smaller articles are afloat, except my shoes. The door entirely disappears and a new one is opened in the floor

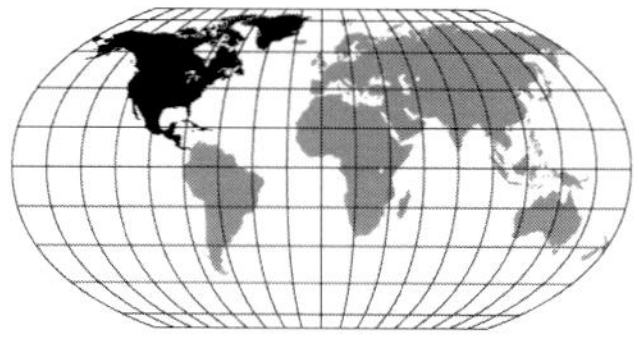

people sailed that year.

Sea-borne trade with North America has been constant since the 1660s. Walter Raleigh had famously imported the first tobacco in the 1580s, and by the 1660s tobacco was in high demand; Liverpool merchants were importing the leaf, and exporting people to run and work on the plantations. Bryan Blundell, for instance, made his fortune in the tobacco trade, though it was not easily made, what with England being at war with France; travelling in convoy with warships provided some protection on the seas, but not much.

An extract from his journal of 1706: 'Left Liverpool in January; had six weeks to Virginia .... In September we sailed from thence. Having for our convoy, the *Greenwich* (James Jason, commodore) the *Woolwich*, the *Hazardus*, a French ship *Prize*, and the *Advice*, with 230 sail of merchant ships. The greatest fleet that ever went out of Virginia, but our careless commodore soon made them fewer, for many left the fleet by his ill-management and several foundered. We were, of Liverpool ships in the fleet, 25 sail, so that I thought tobacco could not be worth much at Liverpool, so made the resolution ... to go for Harwich and dispose of our tobacco for Holland.'

Atlantic storms scattered the fleet, and on 9 November a French privateer boarded Blundell's ship, took it as a prize, and eventually landed Blundell and his crew at St Malo, from where they made their way home to Liverpool on 14 January 1707. A whole year gone with nothing to show for it.

Blundell stopped going to sea in 1714. A religious person, he was Mayor of Liverpool twice and administrator of the Bluecoat School, of which he was one of the founders in 1715, paying for much of the school building.

He has been linked with slavery – not as a slave trader, but because he traded in tobacco, and tobacco was handled by slaves. But Blundell traded in northern Virginia, and there seems to have been very few – if any – slaves in the area before 1712.

As well as tobacco and sugar, grain, fruit, whale oil, timber and furs were all American imports; from Liverpool, ships took mostly manufactured goods, including cloth, pottery – and prefabricated churches.

These cast-iron building kits, exported all over the world, were the innovation of John Cragg and Thomas Rickman – St George's Everton and St Michael's-in-the-Hamlet, Aigburth (along with several houses nearby) are the first examples of their work.

But the king of American trades, from the first bale landed in Liverpool in 1709 to the present day, was King Cotton. From fortune to famine, Liverpool and Lancashire history is woven in the stuff.

In January 1842 Charles Dickens sailed from Liverpool on his first voyage to America, on board the steamship *Britannia*. They sailed through the worst storms for years, as he later recalled:

'The vessel throbs like a strong giant that has just received the breath of life; the two great wheels turning fiercely round for the first time; and the whole ship, with wind and tide astern, breaks proudly through the lashed and foaming water.

'It is the third morning. I am awakened out of my sleep by a dismal shriek from my wife, who demands to know whether there is any danger. I rouse myself, and look out of bed. The water jug is plunging and leaping like a lively dolphin. All the smaller articles are afloat, except my shoes. At the same time the door entirely disappears and a new one is opened in the floor. Then I begin to comprehend that the state room is standing on its head. Before it is possible to make any arrangement at all that is compatible with this novel state of things, the ship rights. Before one can say "Thank heaven!" she wrongs again, and so she goes on. Staggering, heaving, wrestling, leaping, diving, jumping, pitching, throbbing, rolling and rocking until one feels disposed to roar for mercy.

'A steward passes.

"Steward!"

"Sir?"

"What is the matter? What do you call this?"

"Oh, rather a heavy sea on sir, and a head wind."'

the americas

A female crack shot and scalp hunter, Ann Dennis, born in Liverpool in 1742, was kidnapped at the age of 19, taken to Virginia and sold into bondage as an indentured servant. She married a soldier called Bailey, who was killed by Indians at the battle of Point Pleasant. Ann's thirst for revenge drove her to become a scout and messenger on the Virginian frontier. In 1791, when Fort Lee in Charleston was under siege, Ann rode 120 miles, on her black horse Liverpool, to another fort to get ammunition and soldiers. Mad Ann's Ridge in Alleghany, New York, is named after her, and she is remembered in song and with monuments.

The 2,118-ton square rigger *Wavertree*, built in Liverpool in 1885, is in New York's South Street Seaport Museum.

In 1807 Moses Liverpool and a group of other freed slaves built the first school for black children in the District of Columbia.

The crossword was invented by a Liverpool emigrant, Arthur Wynne. The first 'word-cross' appeared in a New York paper on 21 December 1913.

The word 'skyscraper' has Liverpool origins: the skyscraper was the extra top-most sail on Liverpool clippers. As the ship rolled and pitched, the sail seemed to scrape the sky.

At first, raw cotton was brought back from the colonies on the third leg of the triangular trade, bought with profits from African slaves. Cotton garments and goods produced in Lancashire mills were then exported to Africa.

In 1757 Liverpool saw the first recorded cotton auction. The inventions of Arkwright, Hargreaves and Crompton, which revolutionised the Lancashire spinning industry, meant that by 1795 Liverpool was receiving the lion's share of the 17,000 bales imported into Britain. The first imports were of West Indian and American cotton, but from 1810 Egyptian and Indian cotton were coming on to the Liverpool market.

The disruption to the cotton trade caused by the American Civil War caused the cotton famine in Lancashire. The few Liverpool clippers that broke the blockades brought in cotton cargoes that sold at wildly inflated prices; when the war ended prices plummeted. Two Liverpool banks went bust, wealthy traders went bankrupt. In 1862 a mere 72,000 cotton bales were imported (compare this to 1860, when 2.5 million bales came into Liverpool). The cotton famine lasted for four years; in Burnley, for instance, 10,000 out of 13,000 mill workers were out of work and starving; in all, half a million were destitute. In 1863 the city of Philadelphia sent clothing and 5,000 barrels of flour on the barque *Achilles*, 'for the relief of Lancashire distress'.

With the transatlantic trade halted, Liverpool's traders had to look elsewhere in the world. It was John Gladstone (father of Prime Minister William Gladstone) who first explored the potential for cotton in the East Indies. In 1814 his ship, *Kingsmill*, was the first Liverpool ship to sail to India after the East India Company's monopoly was broken.

The risks of transatlantic sailing meant that early news of a ship could make the difference between profit and loss; it was cotton money that had the lighthouse built at Hoylake, and set up Bidston as a flag station to warn of a ship as soon as it was sighted off the Bar. Cotton, again, was one of the driving forces behind the Liverpool–Manchester railway in 1830.

Distance was risk; given the length of time it took to sail back from the United States with a cotton cargo, the merchant could lose a small fortune. Between buying the cotton and the ship docking in Liverpool, the price could drop and force the merchant to take a loss.

Two factors made the trade more sophisticated: the first transatlantic telegraph cable in 1866, and John Rew. Liverpudlian cotton trader John Rew came up with an ingenious solution – hedging. News of any purchase made in America could now be wired straight back to Liverpool. On receipt of the news, Rew immediately sold the same amount at the same price in Liverpool. Then, if the price did drop before his ship docked, he was covered.

The cotton famine made half a million workers destitute. In 1863 the city of Philadelphia sent clothing and 5,000 barrels of flour, 'for the relief of Lancashire distress'

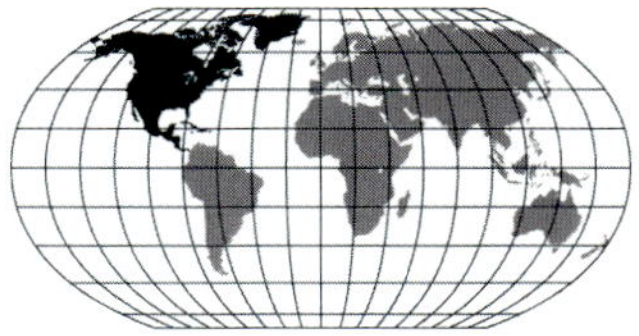

The technique of hedging was adopted by traders in all Futures markets, and the current complex trade in derivatives has taken Rew's invention a quantum leap further on.

The Liverpool Cotton Brokers' Association was established in 1841; cotton traders took offices in the Albany when it was built in 1856, as well as basement rooms around the courtyard where they could display samples. When Liverpool's Cotton Exchange was built in 1906 and traders abandoned the Flags for the weatherproof building, it was not only the first in Britain, but the most advanced exchange in the world of its type, with a transatlantic cable direct to the New York Cotton Futures Market. The Old Hall Street building was a demonstration of Liverpool's wealth, and boasted lavish hospitality. For one banquet 200 waiters travelled up from London on a specially chartered train, bringing with them six turtles and 200 pheasants to tickle the taste buds of the cotton traders.

At its peak, in 1911, Liverpool's Cotton Exchange imported five million bales and held one million in stock: the city was the world's greatest market for trade in spot cotton. The trade declined over the coming decades, and control was ceded to London. Even the old Cotton Exchange was demolished, making way for an altogether inferior building.

Though no raw cotton comes through the port any more, and Liverpool's Cotton Exchange is no longer the focus of the world's trade, the Association – with members in over 60 countries – is still the forum for traders. Almost 70% of the world's raw cotton for export is still sold under Liverpool arbitration.

The South Atlantic meets the shore
Port Stanley, Falkland Islands

chapter two

broadbent garden

101 - 111 Old Hall Street

Three practices; BCA Landscape, Broadbent Artworks and Smiling Wolf collaborated to develop a place to relax, explore and admire the view. The project – part urban landscape, part public artwork, celebrates Liverpool's diverse genepool and far-reaching maritime links.

LIVERPOOL – THRESHOLD TO THE END

Morse

THE TRANSFORMATION OF THE SPACE FROM DAY TO NIGHT IS STUNNING

making it happen

"It would have been far easier for each design team to have gone back to their respective studios to produce their own bit, but we decided at an early stage to work collaboratively and push each other creatively. We knew we wanted to create something unique that we would all be proud to be associated with."

Andy Thomson, BCA Landscape

"This team of three Liverpool art and design practices have believed for some time that we could work together to make something remarkable, and we are delighted to have had this opportunity to test it. Together I believe we have created something quite remarkable, a unique public space that makes real connections to the site and the city."

Stephen Broadbent, Broadbent Artworks

"For us, creating something of great permanence and scale proved wonderfully exciting: Seeing the team's graphic doodles and concepts made into a physical reality (bigger than an A3 poster!) was also thoroughly engrossing... can we do some more please?"

Simon Rhodes, Smiling Wolf

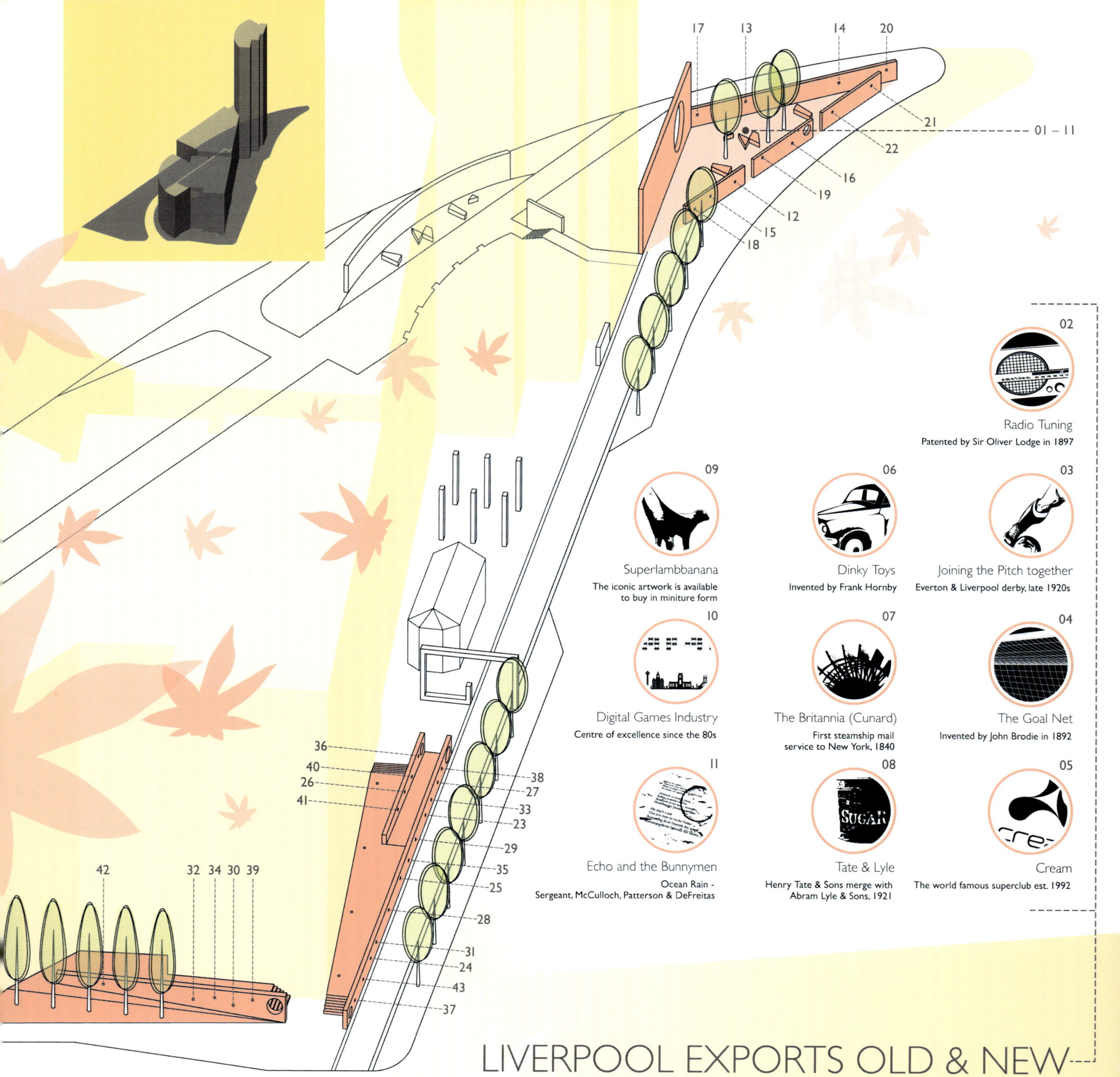

LIVERPOOL EXPORTS OLD & NEW

17

Lynda Bracey
1944 Russia

13

Freda Juckes
1972 Mauritius

14

Jessica Douglas
1982 China

20

Barry Owen
1942 Wales

21

Cathy Tyson
1965 Trinidad

22

Dr Andrew Zsigmond
1965 Hungary

16
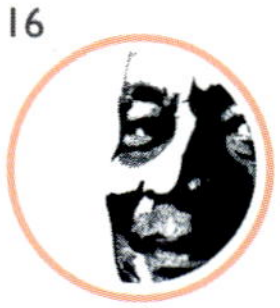
Rudolph Murray
1933 Barbados

19

Zane Billal
1937 Yemen

12

Saranda Hajdari
1989 Kosovo

15
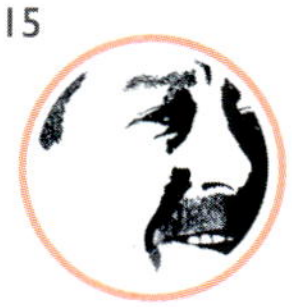
Frank King
1950 Japan

18

Pat Roberts
1950 Spain

38

Pauline Speak
1947 Ireland

27

Julien Hock Toh
1995 Malaysia

33

Dr Athanassios Migos
1959 Greece

23

Michael Vangen
1944 Norway

29

Joan Hogan
1925 Jersey

35

David Beecham
2003 France

25

Madhu Kakar
1948 India

28

Teresa O'Brien
1933 Philippines

31

Kyria Loyden
1983 India

24

Emmanuel Muanda
1973 Democratic Republic of Congo

43

Adriana Noemi Stewart
1964 Argentina

37
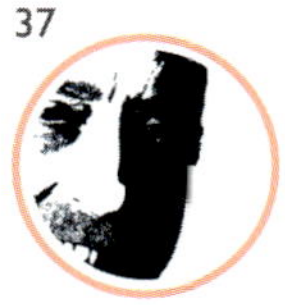
Frank Santangelli
1950 Italy

39

Erik Bichard
1960 USA

30

Mary Maxwell
1939 Ireland

34

Ethan Frost
2003 England

32

Stephen Yip
1955 China

42

Louise Douglas
1974 USA

36

Shirley Mashiane Talbot
1940 South Africa

40

Eddy Amoo
1952 Ghana

26

Irene Cole
1944 Gambia

41

Bill Baker
1940 Jamaica

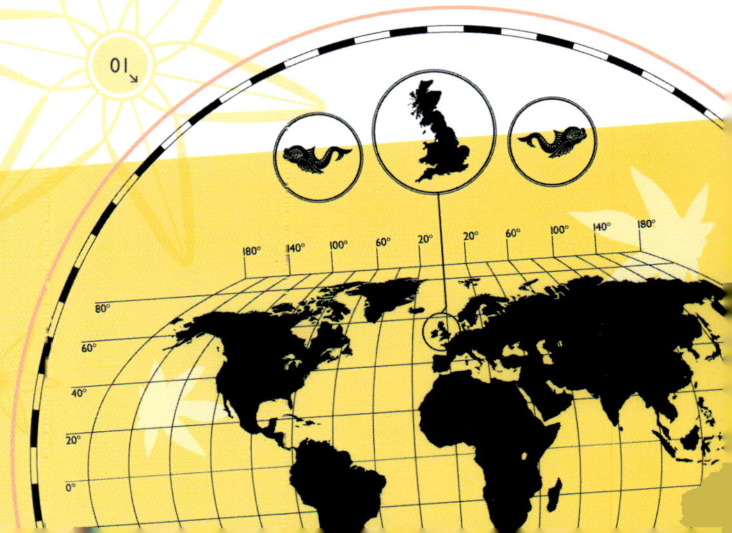

FACE OF LIVERPOOL

Face of Liverpool
No.17 LYNDA BRACEY

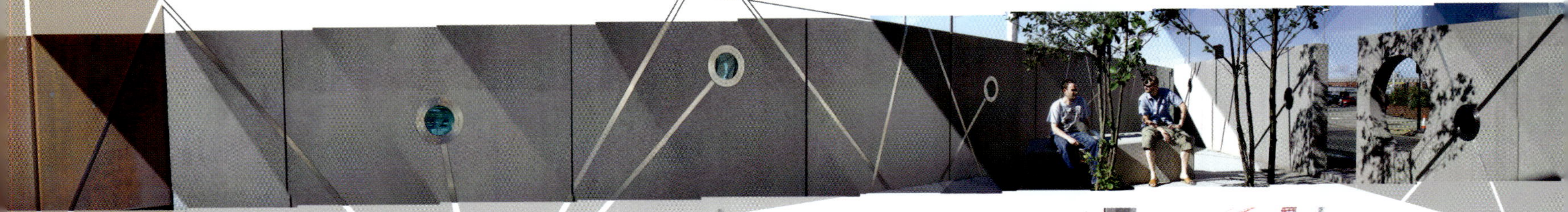

Alnus cordata (Alder)

MORSE CODE PLAZA

3m high faceted cast concrete wall and up-lighters at the base of Beetham Tower. Five bespoke cast concrete seats. Cast concrete Morse Code dots and dashes. Cast aluminium Morse Code key. *Lonicera* (Honeysuckle) groundcover. Resin bound Addastone paving with embedded stainless steel *Liverpool Connection* strips.

CORTEN WALL

6m high corten steel wall with wash lights. 4m diameter hardwood timber window. *Hebe Sutherlandii* groundcover. Michael O'Mahoney 1931 quote "Liverpool - Threshold to the Ends of the Earth". *Liverpool Connection* lines in corten.

TRIANGULAR GARDEN

Alnus cordata (Italian Alder) multi-stem trees with uplighters. Five unique cast concrete seats. 22 illuminated coloured glass portholes – including eleven *Liverpool Exports* and eleven *Faces of Liverpool*. stainless steel *Connection* strips in cast concrete walls and resin bound floor. Porphry stone paving.

Morse Code 'International Port 34690'

COTTAGE FRAME

6m high corten steel frame to converted Leeds-Liverpool Canal cottage. Illuminated coloured glass strips with screen printed 'Nineteenth Century Comic-Strip' – *The Black Prince and the Coffee Bean*. Unique hardwood timber seat. 21 illuminated *Face of Liverpool* glass portholes. Five *Carpinus betulus 'Frans Fontaine'* (Hornbeam). Seven *Acer platanoides 'Emerald Queen'* (Norway Maple) 2.2m high walls and platforms to Passport Office.

post

industrial geology

The ideas that underpin the design are communicated through each element of the landscape. Intersecting lines within the floor and walls create an abstracted three-dimensional map of space and time, highlighting connections between generations and across oceans. Simple geometries, symbols, maps and text evoke stories of travel and adventure.

"The stuff we left out was just as important as that which stayed, all the research and early work undertaken before anybody picked up a pen gave us a series of shared contextual reference points. Once we felt we understood these cultural, historical and physical jigsaw pieces, we then set about using them to recreate and reinvent the landscape. The design process was a constant challenge, but always fun."

Andy Thomson, BCA Landscape

The BLACK PRINCE *and the* Coffee Bean

DISCLAIMER

This is the story of a South American Coffee Bean and its journey to Northern England in the 19th century. Please be aware that some of the characters and events in the tale are almost entirely factual and can be judged as containing educational value.

1

Built in Maryport, Jacksonville Florida, in 1838 and owned by J. Clint & Co., merchants of Liverpool – *The Black Prince* was a 298 ton wooden sailing ship that traded with South America via the dangerous waters of the Cape Horn.

Edward, dubbed the *Black Prince*, was an able warrior with notable victories over the French at the battles of Crécy and Poitiers in 1346, aged just 16. He never ruled as King, dying in 1376 a year before his Father, King Edward III.

2

Coffee growing was introduced to Brazil during the 18th Century, Liverpool's trade with South America began the following century. The highest quality bean is the *Arabica*, and the best flavour is obtained from plants that grow at high altitudes.

The Coffee bush produces a *Jasmine*-like mass of white fragrant blossom, followed by coffee "cherries" which are then picked when ripe. Each of these cherries contains two beans that are ready to process.

Freshly harvested coffee is taken to the mill within hours. The beans, when extracted from the cherries, are soaked and left to ferment. Next they are washed and laid out to dry slowly & evenly. The best coffee is sun dried.

The processing yields *green* beans which are flavourless until roasted. These are graded and packed into sacks for exporting. Our bean is now ready for the long and often dangerous journey across the seas to Liverpool and, ultimately, other parts of England...

GECKO BEAN · CAFE DE BRASIL

3

The voyage to South America, especially navigating the seas around the Cape Horn, was notoriously dangerous. Storms, strong currents and mighty winds became part of seafaring legend; Many lives and ships were wrecked at the infamous peninsula.

Cargo Types

Oranges

Lemons

Chillies

Chillies

Various Meats

4

THE PORT OF LIVERPOOL

Liverpool Shipperies Exhibition, 1886

OLD FAITHFUL TOBACCO
LONDON • PARIS

By the 1850's Liverpool's booming trade industry made it the British Empire's second main port after London. In 1880 Liverpool officially became a city, the following year its' population had reached 611,000 – the city had become a trading powerhouse.

ON SALE

50 Pipes of Port WINE
On moderate terms ;
Also a quantity of Oporto CORKWOOD.
By Kearsley and Bower, 7, Rumford-st.

CONSTANTLY ON SALE
A large assortment of ANCHORS, madeof th best Shropshire Iron ;
CRANE CHAINS, MOORING CHAINS, IRON HURDLES
J Kearsley and Co. 7, Rumford-st.

NEW FRUIT
BLOOM RAISINS, in Boxes,
LEAXIS and SUNS, in Barrels,
GRAPES, LEMONS, ALMONDS
Blocks and Slabs of Statuary and veined Italia MARBLE ;
Real Gorgona ANCHOVIES
Half Chests, SALLAD OIL,
Parmesan CHEESE, CANE REEDS,
And 30 Butts Malaga WINE,
Apply to James Aikin, and Co. or
Percival, Hodson, and Co. Brokers.

Adverts from THE LIVERPOOL MERCURY early 19th Century

During this time Liverpool was bustling with merchants and sailors. All kinds of exotic goods were bought and sold at the docks; Fortunes were made from the cargo of distant countries – the city was synonymous with enterprise.

SIR JOHN LAIRD
BUILDER OF SHIPS

5

The Leeds and Liverpool Canal was started in 1770 to increase the traffic of imported cargo inland, whilst improving the export potential of the booming textile, cotton and wool trades from Lancashire and Yorkshire, to wider regions.

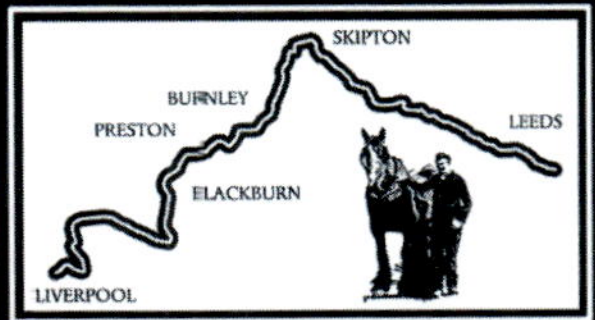

When finally completed in 1816 the waterway gained the accolade of longest canal in Britain. Totalling 127.25 miles with 92 locks and rising to a summit of 487.5 feet above sea level, the canal is a fantastic feat of engineering.

PRINCESS

An elaborate decorative paintwork style emerged for these barges – intricate details, bold colour and highly stylized lettering were all popular features of the time.

A particular type of barge was built to navigate the waterways – *Short Boats*. 60 feet long and 14 feet wide, a little slower but capable of carrying more cargo than a typical narrow boat, with additional space for a bigger below deck living cabin.

6

THE COFFEE HOUSE LEEDS

"Coffee is the common man's gold, and like gold, it brings to every man the feeling of luxury and nobility"

Coffee houses of the time were busy, bustling taverns that were celebrated and condemned. By 1879 3000 coffee houses existed in Britain. They were both social and business hubs, frequented by everyone from writers and artists to merchants and politicians.

The tale of the Coffee Bean ends here.

The coffee houses were now in decline after their heyday in the previous century. Britain's favourite beverage was now under attack from another exotic import – Tea.

The Black Prince ship traded with South America until 1874 when she was sold to carry coal along the coastline of Britain. It is believed that she was broken up for salvage in 1890.

The canal itself has undergone a revival as a focus for the leisure and housing industries.

A statue of Edward exists in the centre of Leeds today. The inscription reads:

Edward Prince of Wales surnamed
The Black Prince, the hero of
Crecy and Poitiers
The flower of England's chivalry
the upholder of
the rights of the people
in the
good parliament
1330 – 1376

The End

goodnight

We wanted the space to be accessible and for people to engage with it, but at the same time we didn't want to limit individual interpretation. So a lot of the thinking is abstracted and impressionistic. The main ideas that underpin all the elements of the design involve geography, distance and how we all have an overriding desire for human connection.

We also believe that 'public places' can provide an inspirational backdrop and setting for shared experiences and chance meetings.

Andy Thomson – BCA Landscape

chapter three

the faces of liverpool

Trinidad
Cathy Tyson

The daughter of a Trinidadian barrister and an English social worker, Cathy Tyson represents many of the people born and brought up in Liverpool whose parents' ethnic links reach to the corners of the globe.

She trained at Liverpool's Everyman Theatre, a cradle in the 1960s and 1970s of many high profile theatrical careers, on and off stage. Cathy's first major film role, playing opposite Bob Hoskins, as Simone in Neil Jordan's *Mona Lisa*, won her plaudits around the world, with BAFTA and Golden Globe nominations.

Cathy is one of Liverpool's well-known faces, and as such was the perfect person to launch the Faces project in 2004. Uniquely in the line up of 32 Liverpool faces, Cathy is the only one not living in the city, and so she represents the multitude of people who have taken a little bit of Liverpool out to the world.

Other actors with Liverpool roots, either themselves born in the city or with Scouse parents, include Kim Cattrall, Halle Berry and Mike Myers; Christine Tremarco (a good Liverpool Italian name); two Harry Potter villains, Jason Isaacs and Ian Hart; classic silver screen smoothie Rex Harrison and the list goes on.

Liverpool has exported many remarkable individuals, some of whom are mentioned in the first chapter, and as the world continues to shrink, Liverpool will continue to exchange talent and human potential as it always has done.

The American poet Allen Ginsberg declared, in the mid-1960s, that 'Liverpool is at the present moment the centre of the consciousness of the human universe.'

As the psychologist Carl Jung put it: 'Liverpool is the pool of life.'

Disco

Ghana

Eddy Amoo

As a member of the band the Real Thing, Eddy Amoo famously wrote and sang about his upbringing in Liverpool 8.

His father came to England from the Gold Coast (now Ghana), first to London then to Liverpool, to escape the outbreak of World War 2. His mother is Liverpool-born – in the Mount Pleasant workhouse, in fact – to an Irish mother and a father also from the Gold Coast.

'I didn't find this out until the last few weeks of my dad's life, but it sounds like he stowed away on a ship to England, like lots of Africans did at the time,' says Eddy of his father. 'He might have taken money from his family and done a runner. In later years I always offered to take him home, but he always refused. Then it became clear why he might not have wanted to,' he says with a smile.

Offie, Eddy's father, became a merchant seaman in Liverpool and married his landlady's niece. Eddy's mother grew up passing herself off as a South American to disguise her blackness and find work. His grandparents had six children, and many of his aunties married mixed race men. 'I grew up in a big extended family. We were all brought up together until we were about nine, when we started to get housed separately.'

To escape the crowded conditions at Tennyson Street, Eddy's mum moved her branch of the family out to live in a cellar kitchen, and sent Eddy to Colomendy, a boarding school in North Wales.

'At first, it was very traumatic. I'd never seen so much green, so much countryside, but we all settled in after a couple of weeks. It was OK, we were all underprivileged kids. There were no racial undertones – if anything it was more about religion. Evertonians and Liverpudlians, Catholics and Protestants.'

By the time he came home, the family had been rehoused in Myrtle Gardens, where Eddy lived from the age of 11 till he was 23. 'I remember my first sight of the flat, and saying to my mam "is this really all ours?"

'It was the first time I found out about being black. I refused to go out, and I'd sit in the yard in the front, and these kids would run up and call me names like "nig nog". Then, one day there was a knock at the door and about eight kids were standing there waiting to take me to the pictures with them. I was horrified, and refused, but my mam made me go.

'I never looked back, and that was the end of it. It was a very happy place. We all got on, the whole community. Looking back at those kids, I don't even think it was a racial thing, I think it was just because I was different, and they didn't know how hurtful they were.'

Offie Amoo was a tap dancer, and played his Hi Life guitar around the pubs and clubs in Liverpool 8. 'I would often listen to my dad playing his Hi Life late into the night. He was a typical working class man; everything would go into the pawn shop on a Monday and was taken

John, Paul, George and Ringo had gone to buy hamburgers. When they heard us sing, they all came running back...

There were no racial undertones – if anything it was more about religion: Evertonians and Liverpudlians, Catholics and Protestants

out again on Fridays. His guitar was about the only thing that never went in.'

Music played a huge part in Eddy's life. He says: 'I guess given my dad's history I was always going to be a muso. My mam took me to the Empire when I was 11 to see Frankie Lymon and the Teenagers. That was it for me. On the way home I told my mam I was going to be famous and appear at the Empire one day. She smiled...'

Eddy and a group of friends formed the Chants in 1962. Liverpool's formidable social reformer, Bessie Braddock, saw them rehearse at Stanley House (L8's social club, youth club and community hub) and took the young band under her wing. Aged 18, Eddy and the band were whisked off to play at the Royal Albert Hall and taken on tours of the House of Lords and the House of Commons.

The Chants auditioned for the Beatles at the Cavern after meeting Paul backstage at a Little Richard gig in Birkenhead's Tower Ballroom. Paul told them to come down to the Cavern when they had returned from Hamburg's Star Club. 'We went down to a lunchtime session; Paul remembered us and we got on stage to sing. John, Paul, Ringo and George had all gone to the back of the club to buy hamburgers, and when they heard us sing they all came running down, and were transfixed. We went back that night, but Epstein stopped us in our tracks, saying "my boys don't back anyone". Paul and John overruled him and we went on stage. Epstein signed us on the spot.'

Despite Liverpool's music scene being predominantly white, Eddy says the Chants found it very easy being black, when all the other musicians were aiming

Fishermen bring their catch ashore at Elmina, Ghana

for doo-wap influenced sounds. ‘We were singing five-part harmonies, doing what the others wanted to do but couldn’t.’

In the year after the Chants started working with the Beatles, the Fab Four went from strength to strength, having their first hit in 1963 with *Please please me.* ‘It was a magic time,’ says Eddy, ‘but the most awful mistake we made was thinking we were stars.’

They changed management, believing Epstein was only interested in the Beatles and Gerry & the Pacemakers, and released a new single, *I don’t care.* ‘We had tabs in the shops – we had a single out – so we thought we’d automatically go into the charts and become stars. Boy, did we get brought down to earth.’

Eddy served a 13-year apprenticeship with the Chants, before realising that the band were going round in circles, performing cover versions rather than the socially aware protest songs they were beginning to write.

Eddy passed his new songs on to his younger brother Chris, who was starting his own band with some of his childhood friends. Tony Hall saw the band and was excited by Chris’ voice. Eddy remembers: ‘Tony was about as big as it gets in black music. He was a Radio Luxembourg DJ, and played a huge part in Motown taking off here.’ Hall took them on and they started with a booking on *Opportunity Knocks.* Just hours before the TV Times went to press, carrying details of the show, Hall was the one who, seeing the huge Coke sign in Piccadilly Circus, christened the band the Real Thing. They won *Opportunity Knocks.*

‘Tony Hall knew the only way to break a black group here was to shake off the American glittery suit image and project ourselves. He thought we had an image which could be developed.’ In 1975, the Real Thing started slowly, but Eddy was

having fun with his music again. Then, one day, music producer Ken Gold walked into their office and played Chris a song which he thought they should record. That song was *You to me are everything.* But, says Eddy, ‘We didn’t like it. It had these sweeping Barry White strings lifted on to it. We’d built up a cult following because we were fresh and outrageous – we didn’t know what to make of it.’

The band didn’t hear anything until one day their manager called to say they were selling 50 copies a day, and then 100 copies a day. ‘But we still thought nothing of it,’ says Eddy. Then a few days later Eddy’s wife Sylvia came running down the road to meet him, to tell him the Real Thing were in ‘the breakers’ – the six records outside the Top 50 that were rising fastest up the chart – and they had a slot on *Top of the Pops* the next day. ‘I can remember sitting there in the dressing room – the Wurzles were next door, who were at Number One with *Combine harvester* – and thinking “How are we ever going to compete with that?” But the day after *Top of the Pops* we were selling 5,000 a day, and then 10,000, and by the time we were selling 30,000 we were at No. 1. It was,’ says Eddy, ‘that easy, and that quick.

‘After we went to No. 1, we went on tour, and playing the Empire was our highlight. As I stepped on stage with Chris that night I was so proud. I knew my mam was sitting there in the audience and smiling, and remembering back to that Frankie Lymon concert all those years ago.’

Their sudden success was ‘like going through the looking glass. You don’t change when you get famous, it’s the people around you that change. But it was the first change for us, the start of a better life. I got my family out of the ghetto.’

Jamaica

Bill Baker

There's not a trace of it in his gravelly Scouse accent, but Bill Baker's roots – his family history – are firmly entwined with the Caribbean islands. His story stretches through the generations, taking in Jamaica, Trinidad, Barbados, and Wolverhampton. His family now are in Liverpool, the United States, and Manchester. It's a true Liverpool tale of seafarers and mariners, of a family at sea, right up until this generation.

'My great-grandfather Abraham came from Jamaica. He was a mariner who settled in Liverpool in the 1870s,' recalls Bill, who, with wife Pauline, has done a great deal of research into the family's history. 'He married a woman called Alice Jones from Wolverhampton, who we think was in service in Liverpool. The 1911 census shows that they owned a boarding house in Upper Pitt Street, with other Caribbean mariners as tenants, and a servant from Dublin. It sounds quite unusual, for the time, for a black man to have kept his own boarding house.'

Abraham and Alice had 12 children; Bill's grandmother Eliza was one of them. And, following in the family tradition, she too married a mariner – her husband Ernest came from Barbados.

'Alice's husband Ernest died in World War 1. He was killed in the Atlantic in 1917, presumably on a convoy from America,' says Bill. But not before they had had three children, Bill's mother Marie, and her sister Alice and brother Robert. Alice married a Trinidadian man. The adventure and perils of a life at sea took their toll on Bill Baker's family: his uncle Bob – another mariner – was lost at sea in the Baltic in the 1970s.

The 1911 census shows they owned a boarding house in Upper Pitt Street, with other Caribbean mariners as tenants, and a servant from Dublin ... quite unusual for a black man

In their family research, Bill and Pauline have uncovered an old family photo of Bill's grandmother Eliza when she was about six years old. 'It's of Eliza with Abraham, over on Bedford Road. My great-grandfather Abraham Lawrence looks like something out of the American Civil War,' he says.

'He's got a large moustache and a bald head, but he's much smaller than I thought he'd be. There is definitely a family resemblance though – he looks like our Matt, dressed up in old clothes.' They've also discovered Abraham and Alice's marriage certificate – which was signed with a cross by Abraham, who was illiterate – and with Alice's beautiful handwriting.

Liverpool's black community is one of the oldest in the UK – many men came here originally as seamen from the Caribbean, West Africa and America. 'There is a strong sense of community in the city', says Bill. But, in spite of their exotic heritage, Bill says his family were Scousers from the minute they settled in Liverpool. 'We all like a curry, but the food we ate was always English, even at

The problem is that when you're young, you don't ask questions, and when you're older, it's too late

White water in the Dunns River Falls
Ocho Rico, Jamaica

my grandmother's. She was the first one I remember – I'd pop in and see her, but I wish I knew more about her.

'The problem is that when you're young, you don't ask questions, and when you're older, it's too late.'

Bill was born in Liverpool in 1940 and, true to family tradition, he became a seaman. He has spent 21 years either on the sea or at its edges, and finished his career working at the Grain Terminal in Seaforth before retirement. He is, he says 'the only one that never got drowned.'

He and wife Pauline have four children, of whom Pauline says: 'None of them go away to sea, thankfully.'

Bill has lived in Liverpool all of his life, apart from those years spent away at sea. He spent seven years as a rigger for the Harrison Line, from 1973–80, and has seen first hand the change at Liverpool's famous docks.

'Liverpool's all changed, especially the docks. When I first started, they were still fairly busy – there was still a lot of work there. There were about 280 riggers when I started. By the time I finished – and was working for the dock board – I think there were six. The docks are doing better than ever for tonnage, but there must be a lot of ex-seamen out there somewhere, spread out all over the place. I always notice that a lot of taxi drivers here are ex-seamen.'

Of course, in years gone by it was the docks that brought so many people to Liverpool, including the Baker family. Abraham's father Dowaney – Bill's great-great-grandfather – ended up in the merchant navy. Notoriously, Liverpool's slavers did a huge amount of trade in the Caribbean, where they sold their cargoes of West Africans – often in exchange for the sugar and tobacco they brought home. Bill and Pauline believe that Dowaney may have been a slave before

joining the merchant navy, as they can't account for him being in Jamaica at that time any other way.

Liverpool was the second city of the Empire, and the principal western port in England. Trade with the East was somewhat restricted by the dominance of the East India Company, whose ships sailed from London, so the trade links between Liverpool and the Caribbean islands grew stronger as increasing numbers of boats left Liverpool for the New World. So, did lots of Jamaicans become sailors and leave the country?

'A few years back people did. A lot of them worked for Harrisons. The Caribbean crews brought sugar, cocoa, cotton, coffee, ginger – all kinds of different things. General cargoes too, before Harrisons branched out into container shipping.'

Sugar, of course, has played a huge part in Liverpool's industry for several hundred years. It was first imported in the 18th century by local merchant Squires, and it inspired companies like Nelsons (who make jam) and the original Everton Toffee to grow around it. Not to mention a little local business called Tate & Lyle, founded by Henry Tate in Manesty Lane.

Even now, 70% of Britain's unrefined brown sugar is imported through Liverpool's docks by a local company, Billingtons.

And Bill has made the journey back across the Atlantic to Jamaica.

'It's difficult to know what to think of it. They advise you not to go out at night – there are a lot of problems there.'

Even though he's taken his family out to Jamaica, he doesn't yet know of any remaining family out there. 'I'm not sure which parish they came from, you see, and there are lots of Lawrences out there – it's like Smith here.'

France

David Beetham

Almost a thousand years ago the first 'English' Beetham was granted an estate in Westmorland; the Norman knight Sir Baldwin de Bethane, who fought for William I at Hastings, held the land for Roger de Poictou, who also owned lands 'between the Mersey and the Ribble'. Before the Normans conquered England, the Westmorland manor belonged to Tosti, the Saxon Earl of Northumberland.

Beetham Hall stands near the river Bela in the south of the county, near Kirby Lonsdale. In some documents the river is written as 'Betha', and its village (or ham) has a variety of spellings, such as Biedun (Domesday Book) and Beithum (about 1200); but there is also the French town Béthune in the Pas de Calais – it has not been firmly established from which source the name comes. The family can certainly trace its lineage back further than the Conquest, to the family of nobleman Ives de Belesme of Normandy.

In 1254 the inquest of Ralph de Bethum showed him to own several profitable estates in what is now Merseyside, at Botele (Bootle), by the Church of St Mary of Waleton (Walton), Kirkebi (Kirkby) and Argarmeles (Birkdale). Half a century on, and Thomas Betham got a charter from Edward II for a market in the village.

Elizabeth Betham, in the late 1700s, married Captain William Bligh, noted plant collector and explorer, perhaps even more noted for being captain of HMS Bounty, against whom Fletcher Christian and others mutinied in 1789. Bligh was later made governor of New South Wales, but again spurred his officers into insubordination with the Rum Rebellion in 1808. What his wife thought of his leadership is not known, but she gave him six children.

Elizabeth's second cousin, Edward Betham, was a remarkable man. Born in Westmorland in 1744, Edward scandalised his father by declaring his intention to become an actor. Had he chosen to be a highwayman, his parents could not have opposed him more bitterly. He was threatened with being disinherited, but Edward would not be turned. He left the Hall, never to return. He even added an extra 'e' to his surname, becoming Edward Beetham and turning his back on 600 years of family history.

A good actor, and inventive with it, Edward came up with a solution to one of the dangers of 18th century theatre: fire. He invented the fire curtain, a roller device raised and lowered on pulleys, coiled on a wooden drum, and stopping the flames of the footlights catching a billowing curtain and starting a blaze. The roller curtain was installed in all the important theatres, but Beetham had not patented his invention, and saw not a penny piece from its success.

When he was 38, Edward came up with the Beetham's Royal Patent Washing Mill, a hand-worked machine which could clean 60 shirts in an hour, and selling for up to five guineas. It made his fortune, and with his clever wife Isabella's success as a portraitist, the Beethams were set for life. At the age of 63, Edward was appointed a director of the newly established insurance company, the Eagle, later to become Eagle Star.

Two centuries later, Edward's descendant Stephen Beetham is helping to make a dramatic impact on the skyline of Liverpool, and his first son David was born on 12 July 2003, taking the future of the Beetham name onwards.

USA

Erik Bichard

Erik Bichard says that his name is a red herring. 'I'm a third generation American, from New York, of Eastern European Jewish stock. Bichard is my step-father's name – he's from Guernsey.'

His own father was Elliot Bindler; all eight of Erik's grandparents had come through Ellis Island from Eastern Europe in the 1880s, part of the last great exodus of the 19th century. From Minsk (in Belarus), Russia, Hungary, Vienna, Silesia – all Ashkenzy Jews looking for a new life. Erik doesn't know their original names – they were mostly anglicised on Ellis Island, where immigration officials wrote down the nearest approximation of a name. So one of Erik's great-grandfathers became Max Bolton; he got a job driving a horse-drawn delivery wagon for Macy's department store.

From Erik's accent there is no way to tell where he's from. It's mostly standard English, with the occasional American twang and now, he says, a Scouse hint, although it's a pretty faint hint.

'I worked very hard to lose my New York accent during my first six months at boarding school,' he says.

His mother had sent him to a Quaker school in Wigton, Cumbria when they arrived in the UK in 1973. 'They'd never seen anything like me,' he says. 'I was 13, with a heavy New York accent, long hair, platform shoes, the lot.'

Wigton, a small country town in the far corner of North West England, close to the Scottish border, was not, in 1973, the most cosmopolitan of places, and tough for a Jewish boy from Greenwich Village to fit in. 'Well, of course, I didn't fit in. Their reaction to me was hostile and often violent; I was pretty badly bullied all the time I was there. As a result I became introspective; it was only after I left and went to school in Saffron Walden to do my A levels that I began to relax and regain my confidence.'

The Wigton school was, he says, the hardest time of his life. A severe contrast with the experimental Village Community School, where his classmates included Gene Wilder's daughter, where he would shoot baskets with his friend's father Elliott Gould, and where Woody Allen was one of the school patrons. 'They were just people's parents. I used to cycle to school past the Bitter End – the club where Joan Baez and Bob Dylan played. I had no idea. It was just typical Greenwich Village life.'

While Erik's father was doing his PhD the family lived in the New York University apartments. 'We were on the 17th floor, facing south, looking over at Manhattan. I watched the World Trade Centre being built. When it was destroyed on 9/11 it hit me very hard.'

Erik was born in 1960, in Westchester County north of NY City; then the family went up to Canada when Erik's father went to study at the University of Manitoba. 'Winnipeg, on the god-forsaken wasteland of the prairies,' he says. There till he was six, Erik remembers baking hot summers and freezing winters, so cold that if you spat in the air it would fall to the ground with a clatter; we'd get snowed in. My mother would make us wear 16 layers before we were allowed outside to play.'

Then it was back to New York. Erik's parents had both grown up in Brooklyn, and although their heritage was Jewish, they turned away from the religion. 'My

His classmates included Gene Wilder's daughter; he would shoot baskets with his friend's father Elliott Gould, and Woody Allen was one of the school patrons. 'They were just people's parents'

mother was convinced that she was a Christian put in the wrong household; in fact she converted to Quakerism in the early 1970s.

'My dad was a rebel and was anti-religion. I wasn't barmitsvah'd or anything – never got into organised religion.

'Although I confess I was quite drawn to the idea of Quakerism: no ministers, no scriptures. But instead I was very taken up with politics.'

Erik's own children – he and his wife Julie have three daughters – all go to King David's primary school in Liverpool. 'But it was almost a coincidence as we live close by. And it has an excellent reputation academically and musically.'

Childwall seems a long way from Greenwich Village; Erik says that he could just as easily have ended up in Italy. His father died, aged 40, when Erik was 10, and his mother got increasingly unhappy living in New York, which she felt was a dangerous, bankrupt and corrupt place to be. 'Ever seen the film Serpico?' Erik asks.

But Erik has fond memories of the city. 'New York opened my eyes to what was possible. My parents used to take me to museums. There was the kids' club at the Museum of Natural History, where we'd get to see live animals, fossils, all sorts. And there were the youth clubs where you could play sports in Central Park, right there in the shadow of the Dakota Building. Fantastic.'

While Erik and his sister were safely ensconced at summer camp one year, his mother went to London. 'She was a free spirit and love to travel. She had a friend in London, at St George's Hospital in Tooting, and also went to see friends in

The Brooklyn Bridge: straddling the Hudson River, linking Manhattan with Brooklyn
New York

Italy. She wanted us all to get away from everything, and decided that we might as well head to London as anywhere.'

So she came home, packed up, and the three of them set off. 'We embarked on the SS France for the five day crossing to Southampton, and she talked her way into the country. We didn't have a place to live, and my mother had no job. Imagine trying that these days. She wasn't as irresponsible as it sounds – she had friends in London, she had done her research, and her chum in Tooting was offering to help her get a job; as an educational psychologist, my mother's qualifications were in demand.'

The family stayed in bed and breakfast in Belgravia for a couple of weeks until they found a flat in Wimbledon. 'I have great memories of exploring the common with my sister,' says Erik. 'Never saw a Womble, even though Mike Batt lived in the same development as us.'

Then it was the nightmare of school in Wigton. 'I was culturally disadvantaged; academically I was a year behind – the Greenwich Village school had been great for encouraging creativity but wasn't so hot on the basics. The history was all different; I had learned Spanish, they learned French.' The only area where Erik could really shine was in acting – he got to the final stages of the National Youth Theatre competition.

After A levels, Erik went to London University for a degree in environmental biology. 'My father was a naturalist, so I've had a lifelong interest in ecology.' He then went to Salford for a Masters in environmental management, then a second Masters degree at Liverpool University, by which time he was a specialist in environmental impact assessment. 'I wanted to get in at the start of thinking behind the built environment. The system lets too much happen too easily.'

A job with Cheshire County Council didn't last more than a couple of years before he went into consultancy. He is now with the Co-operative Bank, heading up the National Centre of Business and Sustainability. 'It's a much broader remit than the built environment – I'm working with corporate boards to help them imagine what things will be like in 20 or 30 years' time. Reinterpret 'success'. Think about environmental and social indicators – corporate social responsibility.'

It's a subject close to his heart. But did his New York childhood have anything to do with it? 'I suppose it had some influence, although I've always lived in cities and enjoyed the closeness of people.

'But consumerism never sat well with me – the waste and injustice of it. I work quite hard to get people to understand that buying things doesn't make us happy. We've become nine or ten times wealthier since the war, but the happiness scale is flat. Having stuff is not the answer.'

What about football, then? Erik is a long time Wimbledon fan – except that since the club has moved out to Milton Keynes, Erik has switched his allegiance to the reformed AFC Wimbledon, which is non-league for now, 'but climbing,' as he insists.

Being a Wimbledon fan created some ripples when he met Julie just after Wimbledon had beaten Liverpool in the FA Cup (1988). 'Her uncles were threatening to beat me up. Jokily. My mother-in-law is passionate about football. My wife and her father are just as passionately against it. Actually it was quite helpful – created an instant rapport.'

So Erik and his growing family are ensconced in Liverpool, despite the two years he spent in Hong Kong after his PhD having 'a whale of a time'. Home is where his family is.

Yemen

Zane Billal

Zane Billal was born in Liverpool just before the Second World War and became a successful publisher, founding Gateacre Press in 1980. He is, he says, the son of two remarkable people, whose extraordinary story is typical of Liverpool's multicultural tradition.

'For my parents,' says Zane, 'it was a love story. They were potty about each other until they died.'

His parents' story begins in the Yemeni highlands in 1923, where Zane's father Ahmed Bilail, a 16-year-old shepherd boy, dreamed of making his fortune in Britain. 'My father had no education,' says Zane, 'but he was highly intelligent, courageous and ambitious.'

The Yemen port of Aden was then a British Protectorate and it was possible to get a British passport and a job as stoker on a ship plying between England and India, then part of the British Empire.

Ahmed and two friends crossed the desert to Aden and talked themselves into seafaring jobs, but the ship that Ahmed joined ended up not in Britain but New York. He jumped ship and made his way to Michigan, where there was a Yemeni community in Dearborn, just outside Detroit – home to the Ford Motor Company. Says Zane: 'My father worked for Ford for about a year, then went into business for himself. I often ask myself how. He had no education, couldn't read or write in Arabic, let alone English. But he built a haulage business and within a few years owned three trucks.'

But, although he had a British passport, he had no American papers, and when the authorities caught up with him he was sent to Ellis Island and deported. He was put on the first British ship out of New York, which landed him in South Wales, at Barry Docks.

Don't tell me that the reason for my life has died. Don't tell me the sun doesn't shine, that the stars don't come out at night. Don't tell me your mother has died.

As in all the deep-sea ports of Britain, Barry had a thriving Yemeni community and Ahmed quickly found friends. But, after almost ten years' hard work in America, Ahmed was once more forced to start from scratch.

It was in Barry that Ahmed met his future wife, Christina, the blue-eyed, 15-year-old daughter of a Danish seafarer. Her father, George Jorgenson, was second-in-command on his ship and was also the ship's padre. The Jorgenson family were very upset about this romance and ordered Christina to give up this illiterate, penniless Arab. Knowing they would not be allowed to stay together in Wales, Christina and Ahmed eloped, with her family chasing after them.

'My parents went first to South Shields and then to Liverpool, where they were married in 1934; my mother was 16, my father 26. By this time my mother had converted to Islam.'

It was soon afterwards that Christina's

He had no education, couldn't read or write in Arabic, let alone English. But he built a haulage business and within a few years owned three trucks

family caught up with them, but seeing that the pair were married and they would not be split up, Christina's family had to make a choice. Says Zane: 'Instead of losing his daughter, my grandfather decided to make friends with this Arab gentleman she had chosen, and my mother and her family were reconciled.'

In the mid-1930s, there were only about 700 Yemenis in Liverpool, but there was a steady flow of seafarers through Liverpool and Zane's parents opened a boarding house and café in Park Lane, near the Swedish Church. Their customers were seafarers and merchants from all over North Africa and the Middle East – the Sudan, Somalia, Eritrea, Yemen. 'It was my mother who learned several languages and some obscure Arabic dialects; she became famous in the local Muslim community and was highly respected. Over 500 people came to her funeral.'

By a strange coincidence, one of the Yemeni boys that went with Ahmed to Aden en route to England, Ahmed Hobarbi, also ended up in Liverpool and, by the time Ahmed Bilail arrived, Hobarbi had become an agent and banker for Yemeni sailors in the UK. Eventually Hobarbi bought a ship, the *Star of Aden*, and went into the import/export business.

Liverpool's Yemeni community thrived and, in 1948, the Yemeni ruling family came to Liverpool to see their countrymen and make gifts to the community. By the Millennium, the Yemeni population of Liverpool had grown to around 9,000: one of the largest in Britain.

Zane explains the difference in spelling between his father's name (Bilail) and his own (Billal). 'The family name, Bilail, means "people of the night"; the family

Behind the wall: the mud brick houses of the walled city of Shibam Wadi Hadramaut, south Yemen

were from a tribe of fortune-tellers. But they did not read or write, so there is no precise spelling. When my father came to England, his name was written down as Billal, so that's now my family name.'

Zane's father, who never did learn to read or write, nevertheless built another successful business in Liverpool with the help of his young wife. Zane remembers a day in 1950 that showed just how successful a business partnership his parents had. 'I used to go to Martins Bank, on the corner of Great George Street (the building is still there), to pay in the takings. This particular day I paid in a cheque for £14,000, which in 1950 was a huge amount of money. It has stuck in my memory all these years – it must have made a deep impression on me.'

As well as the boarding house and café, the Billals had a shop selling a thousand different lines to Arabs, Africans, Chinese, Lascars and Irish (it was a Catholic street); Zane remembers the best sellers were spices and perfumes – great sacks of ginger and frankincense.

The business lasted till the recession of the late 1960s and 1970s, when the south docks declined, the inner city population moved out to the suburbs, and the first supermarkets were opened in the city.

Zane was born in 1937 in the Park Lane house, but was there for only four years, thanks to a German bomb.

'I was four. My father was out on duty as an air raid warden and I was in the cellar with my mother. When the all-clear siren went I, as the man of the house, led the way back upstairs and opened the door into the kitchen. There was blue sky where the back wall used to be: a bomb had fallen nearby and had destroyed part of our house. So we moved a short distance to a house on St James Street, where I grew up.'

Educated at St James Road Cathedral School and the Liverpool Institute, Zane's first job was with the council's treasury; he inherited his father's natural ability as a salesman and sold kitchen equipment, then advertising space, before setting up a business with a partner in 1979.

'I had a heart attack in 1980 and the fairest thing to do was to let my partner buy me out. But I recovered and decided to set up my own business with my wife Christine.'

Gateacre Press prospered, and outgrew several premises before settling in the former Picton Road library, a listed building by the Dutch architect Shelmadine.

Zane is devoted to the memory of his parents, and is still very moved as he talks of their loss.

When they gave up their business in the early 1970s, Ahmed became very ill and took Christina with him back to Yemen for the hot climate, and although Yemen was a strange country, Christina could speak the language and, anyway, could not bear to be parted from her husband.

They were together in Yemen for several years, until Christina got cancer and had to come back to Britain for treatment. She longed to go back to Ahmed in Yemen, but was too ill to travel. 'My mother kept asking me: "Have you got my ticket yet?" and each time I had to fob her off with some excuse. When she died, I had to write to my father to tell him; the letter had to be read to him. His letter back to me said: "Don't tell me that the reason for my life has died. Don't tell me the sun doesn't shine, that the stars don't come out at night. Don't tell me your mother has died."

News of his beloved wife's death broke Ahmed's heart; he died six months later.

HAROLD HOUSE
THE HEART OF THE COMMUNITY
We need your continued support
"Why should I know anything ?
I only work here !"
BUSY?
Safeclean
JJ The Clown
220 2121

Russia

Lynda Bracey

Lynda Bracey is Liverpudlian through and through, and both her mother (born 1908) and her grandmother (born 1880) were born in the city.

Her mother's grandparents, however, had emigrated from Poland; they came to England and Lynda's great-grandmother became cook to a rabbi in London. 'When the family moved to Liverpool, my grandmother was a kind of social worker, meeting immigrants off the ships at Pier Head, translating for them and helping them find their feet.'

In the late 19th century, vast numbers of people were migrating from Europe to the New World. Some travelled to the east coast of Britain and made their way overland to Liverpool to find a ship to America or Australia, but some took ships from Europe. The unlucky ones were dropped by unscrupulous ships' captains who told them, on arrival in Liverpool, that 'This is America'. To find a friendly face who could speak their language and help them would have been a life-saver – quite literally in some cases.

Lynda's father was born in Copenhagen, in 1909; the Danish son of two Russian Jews, he came with them to Liverpool when he was about five and grew up in Anfield. 'At school, the other boys couldn't pronounce his name – Boris Aranofsky – and he was nicknamed Oxy. The name stuck – he was known as Oxy for the rest of his life, although he eventually anglicised his name to Morris Aran,' says Lynda.

(Lynda's married name, Bracey, is also anglicised – her husband's original name was Braslavsky.)

Lynda's father had three sisters; the youngest, Betty, married Bernie Davies and emigrated to America after the war. She still lives in Baltimore. Another of Lynda's aunts, Sadie Roberts, told her the amazing story of her father's parents, Frumke and Velvel.

'My grandfather Velvel was born in Dvinsk in Russia. He joined the Russian army and was posted to a far away town. When they arrived on the train, he fell into conversation with a man on the platform, who turned out to be Jewish. When this kind stranger found out that Velvel was Jewish too, he invited him home for some hospitality. He was then 'adopted' by other Jewish families in the area,' says Lynda.

Through these friends, Velvel was introduced to Frumke, the girl who was eventually to become his wife. Velvel was posted to other towns, but he and Frumke wrote to each other and eventually decided to get married and emigrate.

Life in the Russian army was harsh and Velvel could see the treatment that Jews were being subjected to in Russia. He realised that, if he wanted a good life for himself and his future family, he would have to leave Russia and find a home in another country.

Velvel deserted and headed for a port, where he had arranged to meet Frumke. Says Lynda: 'My grandmother, then very young, travelled alone over hundreds of miles to meet her beloved Velvel and they sailed to Denmark, where they had relatives. It was just like a scene from *Fiddler on the Roof*.'

Lynda knows no other details of the story: 'My Aunt Sadie told me this story just before she died; it's so sad that we don't take more interest in our old people before it's too late. It's so easy to lose

My neighbour lost touch with his brother because he moved to Birkenhead. My neighbour wouldn't even invite this brother to his daughter's wedding

Spring at Petrodvorets – Peter the Great's Summer Palace
St Petersburg

touch,' she says. 'But then you don't have to come half way round the world to lose touch with relatives. My neighbour lost touch with his brother because he moved to Birkenhead. My neighbour wouldn't even invite this brother to his daughter's wedding.'

After some time in Denmark, where three of their four children were born, Velvel and Frumke sailed to Glasgow then, in about 1925, came to Liverpool, where they also had relatives.

Lynda continues: 'They hadn't been here long when they went visiting; their friends took them along to meet another family. To my grandfather's amazement, the "stranger" they were introduced to was none other than the man Velvel had met on that station platform in Russia, so many years ago.'

Despite living in Liverpool for almost 35 years, Velvel and Frumke (whose anglicised names were Wolf and Fanny) never learned to speak English well; they spoke Yiddish rather than Russian, and Lynda's father Oxy grew up speaking Yiddish as well as English.

'My grandparents were very traditional, and I remember celebrating Jewish festivals with them in Yiddish rather than in Hebrew, as we do now.'

Both Lynda's grandfathers were tailors and Velvel, who had a beautiful voice, was also a cantor at the local synagogue.

'My father's parents were devoted; when my grandfather died in 1959 my grandmother just faded away and died a week later.'

Liverpool's Jewish community – the first to be established in the North of England – is about 3,800 strong and a highly organised social group in the city. The community dates back to the early 1700s, when two merchants from the West Indies were known to live in the city. Sephardic Jews, they

were called Leon Villareal and Aaron Baruch Lousada.

There is a record of a synagogue in the city as early as 1753, but it was in the 19th century that the Jewish community became really strongly established as the largest provincial Jewish community in Britain (although this is no longer the case).

Charitable organisation was always a high priority, with the Liverpool Hebrew Philanthropic Society being the first to set up, in 1811, 'to afford relief to poor inhabitants... of the Jewish persuasion during the inclement season of weather'.

Education has been another key to the community's success, with King David primary school dating back to 1841, with the founding of the Liverpool Hebrews' Educational Institution in Hope Place, 'to afford a good plain English education as well as Hebrew and religious instruction'. As early as 1844 a girls' department was opened, and in 1957 King David High School opened in Childwall.

Harold House, where Lynda has worked for 34 years, is Liverpool's Jewish youth and community centre, founded by Harold Cohen for the Jewish Lads' Brigade in 1926. (Cohen was the nephew of David Lewis, founder of Lewis's store.) With a break during World War 2, when the building was requisitioned by the army, Harold House resumed its activities after the war, and became the first Jewish youth club to admit girls. It moved to its current site in Dunbabin Road in 1965; opened by the Duke of Edinburgh, it is also home to the only kosher restaurant in Liverpool.

Open to all, Jewish or not, Harold House is, says Lynda, 'a warm and welcoming environment – perfect for the Capital of Culture.'

Spain

Pat Brand

Pat Brand is the manager of Centec, a regeneration trust in North Liverpool. She has two children and was elected a Fellow of the Royal Society of Arts in 2001, in recognition of her efforts on behalf of her community. She served for four years as an independent member of the Merseyside Police Authority, and for ten as the Honorary Secretary of the Merseyside Fire Liaison Panel. She is on the board of community groups, housing associations, and a member of the Institute of Business Advisers. She is also incredibly modest and didn't tell us any of these things.

Her name offers no clues to her family background, but Pat's grandfather, Jose Rodriguez-Barreira, was a Spanish seafarer. Her grandmother, Julia, was an Irish immigrant, who arrived in Liverpool as a child, fleeing the potato famine.

Jose came to Liverpool from Lleida, a town in northern Spain, between Zaragoza and Barcelona in the Catalonian Pyrenees. Pat has been back to the town since, tracing her family's history: 'It's in a river valley and is just lovely. There are new avenues and modern parts of town and an old cathedral, known as the Seo. The ruins of Zuda are there too – which was the Palace of the Kings of Paragon. It's a site of national importance.'

Jose travelled to Barcelona to find work and became a seafarer. The love affair with the sea remained with him all his life. He continued to go to sea until he was 71 and, even after finally retiring to dry land, worked as a watchman on the docks until his late 70s.

Pat says: 'He met my grandmother on a chance meeting in Liverpool. They were married and he went away to sea again.

In Lleida there are new avenues and modern parts of town and an old cathedral, known as the Seo. But the ruins of Zuda are there too – which was the Palace of the Kings of Paragon

He came and went, as the voyages got longer – he could be away for anything up to nine months or a year.'

He'd often speak to his grandchildren in his native Spanish. Pat remembers: 'The first words I learned from him were the Spanish for "the captain's no good, throw him overboard"!

'He didn't read or write very well in English, but English was spoken at home. He saved Spanish for his cheeky comments. Thinking back, I didn't grasp much more about him than that he was my grandad. It's a bit disappointing really, such a waste.'

Consciously or not, it's a part of her heritage that Pat keeps strong links with: 'I spoke some schoolgirl Spanish, but I'm on a course at the moment, and I'm determined to learn it properly. I don't really know if it's because of the connection with my grandfather, but I suppose that's always there subconsciously.

'I just think it's appalling that, as a nation, we make no effort to speak the local language when we go abroad, and I think it's just plain bad manners if you can't order a meal in the native tongue.'

As grandchildren, we'd fight to go down to the docks to see him and the cart horses. It doesn't seem that long ago

Mediterranean style living in the mountain village of Casares, southern Spain

Pat and her family have visited Spain on holiday, and still have relatives in the south of the country. 'I go out of my way to tell them about my Spanish heritage when I'm there, I'm very proud of it,' she says.

'The Spanish connection is important to my children too – my daughter Frances speaks Spanish very well. In fact, because she's an actress, she wanted to change her stage name to Francesca Rodriguez, but it was already taken. They're very aware of their roots.'

After marrying, Pat's grandparents Jose and Julia settled in Liverpool, where Julia, who arrived here as a child, considered herself very much a Liverpudlian. 'She never referred to herself as Irish at all, although it was there in her phrases, and in her songs. She became very Irish then. But I think it's great to be multicultural. It has impacted on me and I'll always stand up and say I'm of Irish extraction.'

Jose Rodriguez, who was a Spanish Catholic, lived happily in Catholic north Liverpool. 'He settled very well here. Religion was the only influence and he lived in a very Catholic area. He was very comfortable there. He was extremely popular and was always known as Span. It sounds strange now. Maybe you wouldn't be able to call him that these days – but it was just an affectionate nickname. That's how everyone knew him.'

Span remained at sea until he was 71, when he became a watchman on the docks, looking after the cart horses. 'He was very influenced by all the maritime goings-on and knew all the ships going in and out. As grandchildren, we'd fight to go down to the docks to see him and the cart horses. It doesn't seem that long ago. We're fighting for a monument to the cart horses at the moment, in memory of the work they did, especially during the war on the docks.'

Pat Brand was born in Oxford Street maternity hospital and went to St Francis de Sales school in Walton. She worked for United Mersey Supply on the docks when she left school, before training as an aeromedical nurse in the Royal Air Force. She became a student nurse at Liverpool Royal Infirmary before taking a job as a student welfare officer at Liverpool University. She holds a BSc and an MBA – all of her qualifications were achieved after her 45th birthday.

These days, Pat is the manager at Centec, a regeneration centre in north Liverpool. She is a great believer in opportunities and chances for everyone. Centec helps small business get off the ground: it gives them advice, offers them managed workspace, and helps them track down grants and loans to get them started. 'It's a big job, and it can be stressful,' she says, 'but I love it! There's plenty of money around for those that have money, but for some people, it can be really hard for them to get their hands on any. There are all sorts of ways to get hold of the money to start your own business, but many people just don't have the opportunity. We nurture them, and teach them to stand on their own two feet.'

Pat herself is certainly someone who stands on her own two feet, and in doing so encourages others to follow suit. Her daughter, Frances, describes her as 'inspirational' and 'evangelical'. She told us: 'She studied for her degree and an MBA whilst holding down a full time job, running a home and bringing us up single-handedly. She has been a great role model for me and my sister.

'My mum wants to inspire others to aspire. She works so hard for the people of Liverpool, showing her commitment and loyalty to the city that welcomed her grandfather and grandmother.'

Gambia

Irene Cole

Irene Cole is a fifth generation Liverpudlian. She has Irish ancestry, Welsh ancestry, German, Liberian, Bahamian and Gambian ancestors. With her children, and grandson, the family's Liverpool story stretches through seven generations.

Irene's great-great-great-grandmother Elizabeth Clarke arrived in Liverpool from Freeport in the Bahamas. 'She was only about 14 or 15 when she arrived – doesn't it sound young now? She settled in Liverpool and lived here for the rest of her life.' They settled in Beaufort Street in Toxteth, where the family remained for generations. 'Generations now are much more aware of ancestry. Things are better documented and you have things like camcorders. I only have one picture of my great-grandmother, and one of my grandmother, but hopefully my sons will have more of me.'

Irene's grandfather Walter came to Liverpool from the Gambia to study. His father was Welsh, but had married an African wife and settled there, before sending his sons back to Liverpool to be educated. 'It's the Gambian part of the family that I connect most strongly with,' says Irene. 'I can trace our family back there – we've still got a lot of family living there and they've always come over here. There weren't really any customs that we were brought up with as such, we ate African and English food, but my step-grandfather – who was alive until 20 years ago – was a first generation African here, from Sierra Leone, so in my family the African influence is a strong one.'

Her mother Rachel was born in Sefton General Hospital and her family lived in a very close-knit community in Beaufort Street, but Irene is the last generation of her family to remember it as it was. 'It's nothing like it was, now. It's all developed – I'm lucky to remember it – my children don't know it as it was.'

Speke was farmland still... It was so rural. I had a long walk to the bus stop – I'd have to leave the house at about 7am in the morning to get to school

Those communities, she says, were the symbol of a different age. 'People were closer then, they didn't travel, or move around as much as they do now.'

While her mother and her family were all brought up in the Beaufort Street area, by the time Irene and her sisters and brothers were children, the relatives were starting to disperse. 'I remember living in several places – people rented houses. I remember houses on the Avenue and in Parliament Street. My earliest memory of our own home is sharing a big house with relatives – with different families on each floor. Families were bigger and conditions were cramped. You'd be sharing a bathroom, if you had one at all.'

By the time Irene was a teenager, the family had been offered a house in Speke. 'Speke was farmland still, it was just getting developed. I was about 13 when we moved and it was very traumatic when I look back now. In the end I didn't change school, I stayed at Granby Street. It was so

We haven't got the port in its traditional sense so now people come as students and visitors, rather than seamen, like they used to

rural, I had a long walk to the bus stop – I'd leave the house at about 7am to get to school in the morning. Lots of people were moving out of the city centre at the time, but there were no shops, the road-way was nothing like it is now.'

Liverpool's black community is one of the oldest in the country and many families, like Irene's, became well established in and around Toxteth. 'I think the community here is still strong, although not as connected as it has been. People are much more spread across the city, more than they used to be. And we haven't got the port – in its traditional sense – so now people come as students and visitors, rather than seamen, like they used to.'

Irene's father, Tommy Freeman, was – like his wife Rachel – born in Liverpool. His mother was Irish, although her parents were German and his father was Liberian – he'd been brought to Liverpool by one of the Bibby brothers, because he was a methodist. He was put with a family in Liverpool and given a job with Bibby's, where he worked all his life, until well past retirement age.

Tommy became a merchant seaman: 'He'd tell us some tales – the places he'd been to, the conditions he'd worked in. He really had travelled the world.'

Meanwhile, Rachel opened her own shop on Granby Street, and became the first female black shopkeeper there. She was following the family tradition – her great grandmother owned a general store on Beaufort Street, and her grandmother plied her trade from a wheelbarrow... As a child she would sit on its handles to

Golden sands at Kotu beach, Gambia

weigh it down. 'She loved dishes, and china, and opened Ray's China and Glass,' Irene recalls. 'I remember Granby Street as it was then, it got the first Tesco, and there were dairies, a picture house, and a dentist. She was always ambitious. I remember going to the cinema once, and she had an ad in the cinema. People would come from all over to her store, seamen especially.'

Rachel Freeman was nothing if not extraordinary, and very much ahead of her time. 'She did so much community work, her social club was very popular and was a real focal point for the community. She was also the first in Liverpool to have topless barmaids... there were queues right down the road! And she employed a gay barman, which was very unusual at the time.' She opened her club in the 1970s, and it continued to host social events, staff parties and fundraising events. Eighteen months ago – less than a year before she died – Rachel Freeman was awarded the prestigious 'Woman of the Year' title by Cherie Blair, in a ceremony at Liverpool town hall.

Rachel was also an inspiration to her four children. Irene's sister lives in Maryland and works for the Washington Post, her two brothers live in Liverpool – the youngest having just returned here from London, wanting to bring up his children in Liverpool. Irene, the eldest of the four, left school at 15 to become a hairdresser. She says: 'I went for an interview at Peter Collinge (Andrew Collinge's dad). My mum marched me down for the interview, and I can remember hanging back, saying "I won't get that". As I walked in I was the only one in regular clothes, all the others were in their college badges, but she told me I was "just as good as them". And I got the apprenticeship. Andrew Collinge was a toddler, wandering around the shop.'

After graduating from Peter Collinge, Irene left for London, wanting to learn black hairdressing. 'There was no work here. I could do other people's hair, but I couldn't get my own hair done.' Having learned her trade in London, she returned to Liverpool in the sixties and opened her own business, which she ran for more than 20 years.

Irene and her husband were hit hard by the Toxteth riots in 1981. 'Everywhere you looked there were flames,' she says. As key parts of the community, both her hairdressers and her husband's off licence were in the Rialto – the main building was destroyed and had to be pulled down. They both lost their businesses. Her husband went on to own off licences again, in Myrtle Street and Falkner Street, while Irene went back to teaching black hairdressing.

Irene's husband was a Cole – one of Liverpool's oldest black families. Between the Coles and the Freemans, they have created an extended old Liverpool black family... Together they had four sons, all of whom remain in and around Liverpool.

As a mother, she worries about the opportunities available for her sons, and she is adamant that there are still not enough opportunities and jobs, even 20 years after the riots. 'Opportunities are few and far between. You really have to fight for them,' she says.

There is no mistaking the importance of Irene's family to her, and she urges everyone to find out more about their family while they have the chance. 'I never saw my mother as a frail person. I always thought there was plenty of time. Do it while you can – ask the questions, listen to the stories. Families are important.

'Make sure you pass it on.'

China

Jessica Douglas

'I could be described as a true melting pot, with 'Liverpudlian' being the only term to tie me to one place,' says Jessica Douglas, a 21 year old undergraduate at Liverpool University.

Both Jessica's parents were born in Liverpool, but the next generation back leads to quite a diversity of cultures.

'My maternal grandad, Hung Ng, was a merchant seaman from Canton, China. He was on his way to San Francisco but when his ship docked in Liverpool, he got no further,' she says.

'My mother's mother Elizabeth was born in the Dingle, the daughter of a Welshman called Jones from Caernarfon and an English woman born in Liverpool. Her father, from Ireland, was a Mr Hoare.

'Hung and Elizabeth met in the city centre, where my grandad took a shine to my nan and to Liverpool, and decided to stay. They had seven children, and both worked for various companies such as Meccano in Binns Road, just off Edge Lane, and Bryant & May in Speke.'

Jessica's father's parents are of similarly mixed origins. 'My nan, Mary McNally is of Irish/Scottish extraction, as was my grandad Peter Douglas, whose mother was Irish and father Scottish.

'But on my grandad's side there was also French and German relatives with names like Beaumont and von Ecker.'

She laughs at the complexity and admits it's easier to understand if you're looking at a family tree diagram.

Both Jessica's parents, Lynne Ng and John Douglas, were brought up in Speke, which is where they met. They had three daughters, including Jessica, but are now divorced. Jessica lives with her father in Garston.

'There's lots of family,' she laughs, 'and we're very close. There are a few parties every year, as you can imagine. Most of my immediate family still live in Liverpool, but the extended family live all over the world – Hong Kong, China, Australia, San Francisco, Holland, Belgium, Brazil, New Zealand, Bahrain. On every continent, in fact.'

> The extended family live all over the world – Hong Kong, China, Australia, San Francisco, Holland, Belgium, Brazil, New Zealand, Bahrain – on every continent

Jessica, like her two sisters, went to university; she is in her third year studying Human Evolution – a combination of archaeology, genetics, and anatomy. 'I hope to do a Masters, then a PhD, and stay in the academic world. The plan is to specialise in funerary archaeology: tombs and rituals and so on.'

Liverpool has a superb source of inspiration in the Calder Stones, of course, which were part of a rare Neolithic tomb. 'There are Viking remains on Merseyside, too – there has been some work done on the genetic links in Wirral but there is a lot more research to be done.'

Funding for this kind of investigation is hard to come by, which is frustrating.

Liverpool University has an excellent archaeology department – one of the best in the UK, getting consistently outstand-

All the women were aunties; our house was never empty even though I was an only child. Everyone in the area was brought up like one big family

Liverpool's twin: the Shanghai waterfront

ing marks from the assessors. The department is one of Liverpool's best kept secrets, as is the huge collection of antiquities kept in the museum space below Abercromby Square. 'It was established early in the 20th century, while it was still easy for archaeologists and treasure hunters to collect these amazing artefacts.'

Nowadays you wouldn't be given permission to remove such precious things from their countries of origin, of course.

Just as the possessions they leave behind eventually become valuable to archaeologists, so the stories and memories of the humans who made them become valuable in time – but unlike artefacts, memories evaporate with the years, and unless someone in the family takes on the role of local historian and makes determined efforts to record the stories, they are lost.

The story of the Chinese community in Liverpool is hard to research because so few of the Chinese seafarers who came to the city – particularly before the war – could read or write English, although they were usually well educated and literate in their own language.

Jessica's grandfather Hung Ng arrived in Liverpool in the Merchant Navy in 1944 or 1945, towards the end of World War 2. During the 1940s, Liverpool was the headquarters of the Western Approaches, from which the Battle of the Atlantic was controlled; it was also the home of the Chinese Merchant Seamen's Pool, so the war saw a massive growth in the number of Chinese here – up to 20,000 men registered. Many, like Hung Ng, were from the Chinese mainland, escaping the political turmoil in China when the Communists and Kuomintong were fighting.

The Japanese occupation of China's treaty ports during the war stopped many Chinese seamen returning home, leaving them the option of settling in Liverpool.

The irony was that at the end of the war, exactly as had happened after World War 1, many Chinese men were forcibly repatriated, despite having families in Liverpool and other British ports. The government sponsored repatriation schemes were supposed to deal with Chinese seamen who could not be absorbed into the peacetime economy, but unless they had become British nationals by swearing allegiance to the monarch, they were at risk of repatriation regardless of their wishes, or of the length of service in the British navy.

One Liverpool resident remembers a relative whose husband was, as far as she knew, on a six-month trip. But when the money stopped, she discovered that her husband had been deported. She was pregnant, with two children already, and had to rely on her parents for support; the British government recognised no responsibility for the family.

Relatives couldn't always be relied upon. Liverpool-born women who married Chinese men were often ostracised by their families; and when a British woman married a non-British man, they were required by law to register as aliens, losing their British citizenship and most of their rights to welfare support.

In the absence of support from family or government, the women and children of Liverpool's Chinese community built a network of relationships so close – related by blood or not. As one Chinatown resident recalls: 'All the women were aunties; our house was never empty even though I was an only child. Everyone in the area was brought up like one big family.'

In a crisis, women would be more likely to turn to their neighbours rather than go cap in hand to an official agency. The women of Chinatown may not have been rich, but there was no shortage of love in the huge extended Liverpool 'family'.

USA

Louise Douglas

The longest continuous conflict between the United States government and any enemy was not the Vietnam War, but the Seminole Wars, which lasted for 37 years, and took place in Florida. The Seminoles – one of the so-called Five Civilised Tribes of native Americans with the Creek, Choctaw, Chickasaw, and Cherokee – never signed a peace treaty. One of their descendants now lives in Liverpool; but in her sound Scouse accent says she would go home to the Everglades in a hot spit minute given the opportunity.

Louise Douglas, the Liverpool-born features editor of the Liverpool Daily Post, is one of only 5,000 Seminoles now living anywhere in the world. In 1800 there were 50,000.

'There's a tiny Seminole reservation in Florida, but there is a huge number of descendants that no longer call themselves Seminole,' says Louise.

'If I could find the right job, I'd be off back to Florida like a flash,' she says. 'I lived there for a year when I was nine and a big part of me feels that Florida is home.' A subtropical climate with temperatures that rise to more than 100°, a beach ten miles long. And no rush hour. Who could blame her?

Louise's parents met when US Army Corporal Robert Douglas was posted to Burtonwood in 1967 and met Kathleen Connolly at a dance; they married in 1969 then went with the US army to Germany. Then he left the army and the couple returned to settle in Liverpool, where Louise was born in 1974.

The Douglas name goes back to William Douglas, a white man born in Arkansas, who fought in the American Civil War for the Confederates; taken prisoner, he was taken to New York and agreed to fight for the Union. On the USS North Carolina William fell from the rigging, but survived to father 14 children and died aged 100.

Louise's father traces his family back to Richard Taylor, a Creek Indian from Georgia who escaped the infamous Trail of Tears and settled in Florida with the Seminole tribe (Seminole means 'wild' or 'runaway'). By 1830 the population of Georgia had increased six-fold, with white settlers forcing native Americans off their lands; the 1828 discovery of gold in the North Georgia mountains sealed the fate of the Cherokee Nation.

Cherokees in 1830 were not the illiterate nomadic savages as portrayed in Westerns; they were farmers and cattle ranchers, building roads, schools and churches, with a representational government, and the 'Talking Leaves' alphabet. Many took English names and some married Europeans. Despite this, President Andrew Jackson pushed through the Indian Removal Act and in 1838 General Winfield Scott arrived with 7,000 soldiers to begin the forced removal of the Cherokees.

No-one knows how many thousands died from starvation, disease or exposure, on the long journey or while they were trying to settle in the new reservations; 4,000 Cherokees are known to have died, on what became known as the Trail of Tears.

But some escaped – including Richard Taylor – to North Florida, only to find themselves in the middle of the Seminole Wars, with President Jackson determined to push the Indians out of Florida entirely, or at least down into the swamps of the

No-one knows how many thousands died on the journey from starvation, disease or exposure, on what became known as the Trail of Tears

Pier Head, California style: the pier at Santa Barbara

Everglades. The Seminole Wars, or Florida Wars, lasted from 1821 to 1858, between Florida's Indians and the white settlers backed up by the US army. There was a treaty signed in 1823, at Moultrie Creek, but some Seminole warriors refused to sign, seeing the danger ahead. One such, Neamathia, said: 'Ever since I was a small boy I have seen the white people steadily encroaching upon the Indians, and driving them from their homes and hunting grounds. I will tell you plainly, if I had the power, I would tonight cut the throat of every white man in Florida.'

Later, the warrior Osceola declared: 'I will make the white man red with blood, and then blacken him in the sun and rain, where the wolf shall gnaw his bones and the buzzard shall live on his flesh.'

The Seminoles never formally surrendered to the US government, says Louise. 'We are an undefeated people.'

Although Louise can't put 'Seminole' on her passport, she feels very much part of the heritage and takes great pride in her people's history.

Louise's great-grandmother Minnie was a full-blooded Seminole Indian, who married Thomas Criswell in 1905; they had a daughter, Bertha, who when about four months old, was carried off by a bear; the neighbours shot the bear, and Bertha was rescued safe and sound. In 1929 she married Albert Douglas, and their son is Louise's father Robert.

For the Seminole family to use European names was common throughout the Five Tribes: some chose to anglicise their names, some were given English names by lazy census takers – in the 1820s there was a huge census of Indian tribes, and each person was given a roll number and an English name. And there were some who married into European families, English and others.

Unlike the nomadic tribes such as Cheyenne, Sioux and Comanche, the Five Tribes had always intermixed – with Cubans who fished the waters off Florida, with the Spanish who stayed after ceding Florida to the US government, and with the African slaves who fled to the Everglades from the Southern states.

'So we were always told we were Seminole, but we probably have as much Creek or Cherokee blood,' says Louise. 'But I'm told I have the Seminole nose,' she laughs. 'And Dad has the look. Someone in a pub here once asked him if he was Seminole, which surprised him. Most people take him for Mexican, or even Asian.'

It may be cool now to be Indian, but it isn't long ago that attitudes were very different. 'Even 20 years ago it was worse to be Indian than to be black, which in the American South is quite something. My grandmother told me she heard people saying in the street: "There goes old man Douglas's squaw."

'My grandfather Albert remembers as a child seeing a black man being tarred and feathered and dragged through the streets, for having a relationship with a white woman.

For that matter, Kathleen Connolly's father, remembering the GI brides leaving Liverpool after the war, wasn't too happy about his daughter marrying an American, says Louise. And in the end, the cultural differences told. 'My father found he couldn't live over here, so he's now in Florida, and my mum is in Liverpool.'

Is Louise the only Indian in Liverpool? 'I know there was a Sioux who was a welder at Cammell Laird,' she says. 'And when Buffalo Bill came to Liverpool with his Wild West Show a couple of Indians stayed here and married local woman, so I imagine there must be some descendants.'

England

Ethan Frost

First cousin to David Beetham, Ethan – born in May 2003 – is the son of Simon Frost, a director of the Beetham Organization, the family business that has grown from a standing start in Liverpool.

Despite the differing surnames, Ethan and his younger cousin David – like their fathers Simon and Stephen – share a striking family resemblance and a bloodline that stretches back to the time of Tosti, the Saxon Earl of Northumberland.

Stephen's decision to change from his family name of Frost to the older family name of Beetham changes none of the close relationships; Simon and Stephen work closely with their father to build the business and, in so doing, add to the built environment of Liverpool, Manchester and Birmingham, with London and Brighton in their sights.

Hugh Frost – father of seven and grandfather to Ethan – began a small property development business in Liverpool half a lifetime ago; it was in the 1990s, when his sons Simon and Stephen joined him, that the company made a quantum leap to daring redevelopments of existing commercial buildings, and then again to new build projects such as the award-winning Campbell Square development in Liverpool's difficult Georgian Ropewalks area, full of listed buildings long ignored and, occasionally, listing in more ways than one. Narrow streets, infrastructure in dire need of renewal, a vocal group of residents, tenants and landlords wanting the best of every world, a local authority with a very long list of priorities, and funders who needed convincing that this long neglected area offered the potential they were looking for.

Beetham's move into major mixed schemes attracted the usual sceptical carping suggesting that the company should stick to its knitting. But in the true spirit of Liverpool enterprise that runs through this book and the city's history, the Beetham family business proved its critics spectacularly wrong, and in the last decade has leapt on to a national property stage with panache, making the Beetham family motto, 'Per Ardua Surgam' (I rise through difficulties) particularly apt.

To quote the buyer of one of the apartments in the Manchester Beetham Tower – which started construction in early 2004: 'This will be the most stunning block of apartments anywhere in the country; the highest living space. Some people think it is a big risk but I don't agree. It is designed by one of the best architects, is being built by a reputable company, and is in a great location.'

Rapidly gaining a reputation for their striking glass towers on key sites of city centres, Beetham and the Frost family are repeating the success of their first tower in Liverpool, which includes a four-star Radisson SAS Hotel topped by 133 apartments with stunning views, from one side out to the mouth of the Mersey, from where a seventh of the world's trade was once controlled; on the other side of the tower is the view over the rooftops of Liverpool. From the deck of a ship in the Mersey, the Beetham Tower is one side of a frame for the city, echoing the great tower of Liverpool Cathedral to the south.

The garden at the tower's foot is public art that raises the way we look at ourselves, says Ethan's father. 'In art, as in all life, we see what we want to see, and connect with it in our own ways.'

Kosovo

Saranda Hajdari

On 9 December 2004 the Hajdari family were celebrating – that was the day that ended a long nightmare. 'We had a letter from the Home Office giving us indefinite leave to remain,' says Saranda, a huge smile on her face. The legalese means that they are no longer refugees but British residents who in 12 months time will have their British passports.

It has been five years since Ekrem, Nazlije and their five children were airlifted from the teeming refugee camps of Macedonia and brought to Liverpool, with nothing but the clothes they stood up in. Saranda, the eldest child, was 10; she could say 'My name is Saranda' but that was the extent of her English. No-one else in the family spoke a word.

So Saranda became the family spokesperson when the Albanian interpreter wasn't available. All the children but six-month old Irsa were sent to Morrison primary school where, according to head teacher Wilf Roe, they put his English pupils to shame with their hunger to learn and the speed with which they learned both the language and the ways of an inner city British school. Within six months Saranda was fluent, with a distinct Scouse accent; her younger sisters Shqipdona and Almedina, and her little brother Endrit were just as quick to learn, but without as much of the confidence and ebullience of their big sister.

For children who had been through the unimaginable torment of seeing a war rip their world apart, the Hajdaris were sunny, energetic and engaging.

Saranda hurled herself into local life, wanting to meet as many people, learn as much and contribute as much as she could. She loves Liverpool and her life here, although she is passionately patriotic and loyal to her homeland, taking part in social and cultural events and promoting Albanian and Kosovan traditions.

'To come to Liverpool and be given this flat, after the mountains and the refugee camp, was like paradise – like living in Buckingham Palace.'

Despite the impersonally harsh treatment they were to receive at the hands of the Home Office, Saranda says their experience of Liverpool has been a positive one. 'A major reason I felt so at home here was the people. They were really genuine and caring from the moment we arrived, which helped me so much because a new country isn't much use without the people. They are the ones who make you feel secure and change your life.'

Now 15, due to take 11 GCSEs in the summer of 2005 and planning to go the London School of Economics for her first degree, Saranda became one of the first six UK Youth Advisers appointed by UNICEF. She has already been to Belfast and London on UNICEF business, hopes to go to Ethiopia in the spring, and is applying for a more senior role as a Youth Representative.

But while Saranda is considerably more mature and politically sophisticated than her English peers, she is still a teenage girl, and the serious side of life is only a part of her existence. Music, dancing, romance, clothes, celebrities and sport consume much of her time and energy, as it does that of her sisters and her best friend Abulena, a Kosovan girl whose father has had a British work permit for several years.

But overriding everything is her family. There is nothing more important than the

A gentle, softly spoken man, who spent his life working with young children, was accused of terrorism and sentenced to a firing squad, along with over 100 other men

safety and happiness of her parents, her five siblings (including baby Lanika, born in summer 2004) and the extended family in Kosovo. The great sadness of her uncle Mexhid's long illness and eventual death took a terrible toll on them all, especially his brother Ekrem. Mexhid and his wife had lived next door in Liverpool for four years, but in the end they chose to go home for Mexhid's last months. The strain on Ekrem was overwhelming, particularly as it coincided with the climax of their appeals process and a traumatic tribunal in Manchester, in September 2003. As a result, they were given a three year leave to stay, but it has been yet another 15 months to wait for the final, wonderful news of their permanent residence.

To understand what this educated, middle class European family have been through is hard. Not only to imagine the terror, the sense of loss and the huge challenge of restarting a life from scratch in a strange country, but even getting a handle on the almost impossible complexity of the Balkans in the 1990s. Try this analogy.

Edward Smith, an Englishman from Liverpool, and his wife Megan, originally from Llangollen, live in Oswestry, a town on the border between England and Wales. Megan is a fashion designer and has a shop in the town; Edward is a primary school teacher; they have a nice house and a comfortable income. Despite the history of sporadic conflict between the English and the Welsh along the Marches since the time of Glyndwr, the two families are close, the children are happy, and life is good.

Wales has its National Assembly, even though it is a province of Britain and not an independent nation; but then a newly

The red rooftops of Prizren District, near the Albanian border
Kosovo

elected Prime Minister in London decides that Wales should be merged back into the British identity, and sends the army in to quell any rebellious ideas the Welsh may have. There are armed soldiers in the streets who abuse the power they have over the local people and create an atmosphere of constant threat and fear.

Then the Welsh nationalists whip up anti-English feeling and a paramilitary group attacks English families living in Wales, killing some and driving others out of their homes. The Prime Minister sends in crack English troops, who assault Betwys-y-Coed, Ruthin and St Asaph, killing more than 80 people. This spurs thousands of people to join the Welsh Liberation Army and over the next months the violence escalates. The English army destroys villages and towns and forces thousands of people to flee, and WLA extremists attack the minority English residents in Wales, although WLA policy is not to target civilians.

In Oswestry, the Smith family find themselves distrusted by both sides: the Welsh think they are informers for the English; the English see them as troublemakers. An English army officer, Major Richardson, pulls Edward Smith in and tells him he must join the army. Edward signs up rather than risk prison, then goes home and tells his family to pack – they have no choice but to leave immediately.

For Britain, England and Wales, read Yugoslavia, Serbia and Kosovo; for the Prime Minister, read Slobodan Milosevic (now on trial in the Hague for war crimes). For Edward and Megan, read Ekrem and Nazlije. The rest is what happened to Kosovo in 1998 and 1999.

Imagine yourself caught in such a bizarre and terrifying situation: threatened with violence by your neighbours, forced to leave behind your comfortable home and your business, run into the night with your children in your arms, fleeing from other British people who want you dead.

The history of the Balkans is long and extremely complex; the area is a volatile mix of cultures and a political volcano. The Kosovan war has its roots in events of 1389 – more than seven centuries ago. The bloody conflicts of the 1990s in Croatia, Bosnia and Kosovo were the latest in a long series that included the assassination of Franz Ferdinand in Sarajevo, the shot that sparked off the conflagration of World War 1.

In March 1999, NATO launches unprecedented air attacks on Serbia and Kosovo, but the atrocities continued, with huge numbers of ethnic Albanian Kosovans escaping through the mountains to the refugee camps of Macedonia.

As the Hajdari family joined the stream of refugees heading for the mountains and the illegal border crossings, Ekrem was captured and taken away, leaving his wife and children not knowing if they'd ever see him again. Ekrem – a gentle, softly spoken man who spent his life working with young children – was accused of terrorism and sentenced to a firing squad, along with over 100 other men.

By some miracle, Ekrem got away and, by another miracle, found his family in the Macedonia camps. No-one in the family wants to talk about this horrific time; the memories infect their dreams and threatened their sanity. 'It's our past, and part of us,' says Saranda. 'The dreams will be there for the rest of our lives, but we have learned to live with them.'

The courage, dignity and generosity of Saranda and her family, and their eagerness to embrace life to the full and give something back to the city that adopted them, promises that the Hajdari family will be a great asset to this city; we should make the most of them.

Jersey

Joan Hogan

Joan Hogan and her younger brother Alf Whittle are thoroughly Liverpudlian; Joan, born in January 1925, married John Hogan and has three children. She is the eldest granddaughter of Julia Andrew, who was born 80 years earlier and had a long and extraordinary life.

Born Julia le Brun, in St Brelade, Jersey, Julia was just two when her parents left the island with some other Channel Island families. Why they moved, Joan and Alf have not managed to discover. 'Perhaps it was the lure of bright city lights and the prospects of more lucrative work,' Joan suggests, an option which to people living the quiet rural life on a small island in Victorian Britain may have seemed very attractive.

Whatever the reason, the le Brun family came to Liverpool in 1867 and settled in Walton. Julia went to Blackburne House on Hope Street and then, at 21, married Leo Andrew. His father, Henry Andrew, was stationmaster at Woodside railway station for 31 years.

Julia and Leo married in 1886, and had five children – including Emma Hetty, who became Joan and Alf's mother.

The marriage eventually broke down when Leo failed to earn enough to make ends meet, and he left Julia and the children to fend for themselves. Julia, desperate to keep the family together, was forced to go out and find work. 'She found a job with the Elder Dempster shipping line, but it meant going to sea for months,' says Joan. 'She had no choice but to leave her eldest daughter Mabel, then about 14, to look after the younger children.'

So in 1910, at the age of 45, Julia went to sea, on board the Elder Dempster banana boats, plying back and forth to the west coast of Africa. On the first trip Julia was away for five long months.

'We know that in 1920 she was working on board the 4,800-ton *MV Elmina*; she was the only woman in the crew of 115. She was officially down as a steward, but we gather that she was like a nanny, looking after passengers' children.'

There were three Elder Dempster ships called *Elmina*, the first was launched in 1873, the second in 1885, and the third – on which Julia worked – in 1906. Originally named *Albertville*, it belonged to Cie Belge Maritime du Congo before being transferred to the Elder Dempster fleet and renamed. In 1928 it was sold again and renamed *Iphigenia*.

'Elder Dempster were unique at the time, paying men and women the same wage for the same work,' says Joan. 'And the wages were higher than for equivalent positions on dry land.'

The wages might have been higher, but so were the risks.

In her 26 years on the African run with Elder Dempster, Julia was shipwrecked twice, torpedoed twice in World War 1, once off the coast of Holyhead and had malaria twice.

'I believe that everyone whose ship was torpedoed got a medal,' says Joan, 'but we haven't got them, and although we think we know who had them, they're dead now and we can't find a trace of them.'

Quite apart from these extreme events, tropical storms and tornados were normal hazards on the African routes. A typical round trip would take seven weeks or more, and even within sight of the Mersey on the way home, ships could be delayed for hours, even days. There they

In her 26 years on the African run with Elder Dempster, Julia was shipwrecked twice, torpedoed twice in World War I and had malaria twice

Corbiere lighthouse: the first on the British Isles to be constructed of reinforced concrete, 1874
Jersey

would be, hove to and anchored, waiting for the fog to lift, or the gale to blow itself out, or the dockers to call off the strike – or whatever the reason was.

Still, the trip could be beautiful, through clear waters under brilliant blue skies, with flying fish and dolphins tracking the ship. Cargoes would include cocoa, rubber, ivory, palm oil, even gold.

'Julia is renowned for sending back all sorts of exotic goods to her family as well as money; there are family photos with beautiful silk dresses that are said to have been sent by Julia,' says her granddaughter Joan. 'It must have been exciting opening parcels from her, covered in exotic stamps and postmarks.'

After the *Elmina* was sold, Julia joined the crew of the *MV Accra*, on which she served till she retired in 1936. 'She was forced to retire when the National Insurance system came in,' explains Joan. 'They found out how old she really was and retired her immediately.'

Like so many seafarers before her, Joan had lied about her age to get her first job, but instead of the normal practice of adding a few years, she subtracted a whole decade. When she left Elder Dempster she was 71 years old.

Julia retired three years before the start of World War 2, but the *MV Accra* didn't escape the conflict: she was torpedoed and sunk in the Atlantic in 1940 with the loss of 19 lives.

Perhaps Julia's Channel Island blood was what took her to sea.

Always a political possession of great strategic importance, sitting in the English Channel so close to St Malo and the French coast, Jersey belonged to Brittany until 993AD, when the Duke of Normandy seized the islands; when Normandy was taken back by the French king in 1204, Jersey stayed loyal to England. From then on the Channel

Islands were a flash point between the old enemies, and were attacked and occupied by the French in the 1380s and again – this time for seven years – in the 1460s.

Jersey loyalty in the Civil War was divided – the islanders backed Parliament, but the de Carteret family held the island for the king. At the Restoration, Charles II gave George Carteret a large grant of land in the American colonies, which he named New Jersey.

What with the English at war with the French, themselves, the French again, the Americans (and the French) and most recently the Germans, Jersey has been on its guard for most of its history, since the Vikings invaded in the 9th century.

Since the 17th century Jersey seafarers have built up thriving businesses in New England and Newfoundland, and many islanders emigrated there. Fishing boats from Julia's home town of St Brelade would leave the little port after a service of blessing, and head for Canada's east coast on trips of up to eight months.

Jersey was also one of Britain's largest shipbuilding areas, like the Mersey: the island built over 900 wooden vessels.

The finance industry is now, since the 1960s, the major employer on the island, but at one stage knitwear production – of all things – reached such a scale that it threatened the island's ability to produce enough food, so laws were passed, regulating who could knit and when.

Joan hasn't tracked down any family members still in Jersey, although on a trip to Jersey, she found gravestones of some of Julia's relatives in St Brelade.

After her retirement, Julia returned to shore life in Walton with her family; she died, aged 92, in 1957. Joan and Alf both remember her but, says Joan, 'she was just my grandmother. I didn't realise what an life she'd had till I was much older.'

HOME
Numbers

Mauritius

Freda Juckes

'It's funny... my dad's earliest memory of England is walking down the street on his way to art college, looking up, and seeing the Beatles playing on the roof of Apple Studios. He'd been in England about two weeks at the time,' recalls Freddy Juckes. Hers is a story peppered with funny links, coincidences and uncanny parallels – little did he know at the time that his daughter would adopt Liverpool as home.

Today, Freddy still speaks with a trace of an East End accent. She was brought up in London's East End in the 1970s, where her Mauritian father and Irish mother settled together, in the midst of a predominantly white community. Freddy's father left Mauritius for England aged 16, with his mother and two sisters. His father – who ran a printing company – stayed on the Indian Ocean island to help finance their move. The family moved to Mornington Crescent in north London, where Freddy's father went to art college and joined the Greater London Council as a plasterer. He then started his own firm, which went on to plaster many of the covings and cornices of London's palaces.

Her mum left Galway in Ireland, also aged 16. She moved to Bristol, where her older brother had already settled, before joining a teacher friend on a cultural trip to London. They ended up at a Mauritian dance in the Prince Charles cinema in Leicester Square, where she was paired off with the only young man in the room. It was the man she was to marry.

'Mum commuted every weekend after that,' says Freddy. 'She caught the first train to London from Bristol on a Saturday morning, and was always on the last train back. She never stayed the night.' They married aged 19 and had their son soon after, followed by Freddy a year later.

The young family moved to Peckham, moving on to the East End when Freddy was two. 'They had the opportunities in London that they both left home for, and they bought their own house for something like £4,000, which was a lot of money at the time.

'Despite the opportunities, the hardest thing for them was having two mixed race children. The East End was still very white at the time, very BNP. And we had a black dad and an Irish mother. There are some horrible memories – I remember my mum being spat on and called every name under the sun. It never happened when we were out with my father, just my mum. But as bad as it was, the road we lived on was fantastic. You could leave the doors open and there was always a group of kids playing out in the street.'

The East End now is a different place, says Freddy. And it was around the time of the Queen's Silver Jubilee in 1977 that it started to change. 'There were more black and Asian faces around. There were street parties everywhere, so you had to mix. Everyone sat down together – it didn't matter what you were eating, it was just that everyone was doing it together. Suddenly there were kids you'd never seen before at your table – I've got a great photo of us at the time – there are kids of every colour in it. But I just didn't see colour when I was a kid, and I'm hoping that for my son it won't be an issue.

'But race was always an issue. I started to clock the racism when I was about six or seven – I remember my mum being spat on, and I knew the only thing that

He'd sit there and say 'this is really important' and we'd just be thinking 'my dad's a madman'

was different was the colour of our skin. But I wouldn't allow it to upset me – my parents didn't, in fact, I think it pushed them closer together, and they were always very open about it. Their belief in equality made them strong. They were very philosophical about it – they taught me never to treat people on first looks.'

Growing up, the twin influences of Mauritius and Ireland played their parts in Freddy's upbringing, but in quite different ways. 'The Mauritian family were a huge influence... the food, the music... church was the Irish bit. My mum cooked Mauritian food, and she cooks better curry than all dad's sisters.

'Music was a huge passion of my dad's – especially the sega, which is like calypso. Whenever the family came round we'd all get up and dance. It was embarrassing at the time – we just wanted to play with our cousins. But we loved it really.

'Every Sunday after church my dad would sit us down and make us listen to music. Every single type, from Mozart to Little Richard, Engelbert and Bob Marley. And not just for an hour or so, it was a real half a day session. He'd sit there and say "this is really important" and we'd just be thinking "my dad's a madman". But I've got such a love for it now – except cheesy love ballads, which Mauritians love. He taught me to open my eyes, to be up for everything. Mauritians are the loudest people. They'll just shout over the TV and the stereo. It's bedlam.'

The Irish roots too played a significant role in Freddy's and her brother's upbringing, but in quite a different way. 'We went back to Ireland for every holiday, to the family farm. It was as if we'd been let loose. We'd be off with my mum – on the train, then the boat, then the train again. It was a hell of a trip in those days. I remember the first time we went on a plane – it was a big luxury.

'But the farm was like going back in time about 200 years. There were loads of cattle, chickens and pigs, and you'd be hand milking the cows and feeding the calves. There were beehives in the orchards and they'd make their own haystacks, which me and my brother would always destroy. I still don't know how they put up with us. But it was a big thing – we had to behave if we wanted to go away on holiday.'

Mauritian fishermen ply their trade on the Indian Ocean

Because her mother's family were in Ireland, they didn't meet Freddy's father until nearly ten years after her parents were married. 'We'd all gone to Ireland together. I remember mum being really nervous, and they went off down the pub and had too much pucin. When they came back, mum asked something like "is he OK?" And my grandad just said, "apart from the earring". She needn't have worried.'

Freddy was 16 when she had her first taste of her father's homeland. 'Twenty-one of us went out for a cousin's wedding – we went for two months and we had to stay another two weeks because of a cyclone. It was very hot, and it's very beautiful, but having Christmas day on the beach was bizarre – just not right. Going back with my dad is brilliant – he really turns into a kid when he's there, showing us where he had his first cig and where he used to skive off school. He goes on and on about Mauritius when he's not there but, as my brother always tells him, he's lived in England longer than he lived in Mauritius now.'

One of the things that's most striking when Freddy talks about her parents and their families is the number of similarities between them, despite roots thousands of miles apart. 'When we were in Mauritius we had to be careful of things like shrines, because of their superstitions. The Irish are like that too. When you have very little, you're all very much the same. The attitudes and the morals are the same.'

'The first time I ever came to Liverpool it was pissing down. But the two places I feel completely safe are Liverpool and New York. I don't know if it's to do with the docks, or the industry and the immigration. The East End's a lot like that too. Things are moving fast here – it can be a little scary. The Capital of Culture is fantastic, and will have a huge impact, but

I don't want it to be forgotten about after. These things always go in cycles – the East End boomed in the 1980s, but there's a lot of poverty now.'

Freddy has lived in Liverpool for ten years. She studied at London's prestigious Guildhall: 'The only theatres I wanted to work in were Stratford East and the Everyman. The Everyman has just done such great work – it's a theatre for the people, not commercial. It has an impact on the community, and encourages the community to be involved – it's socially responsible. I understood the battle to do really good work.'

She met her husband Abe at her first show, *Blues in the night*, on the first night of the theatre's 30th birthday celebrations, and he proposed after six months. 'I'd been up to Liverpool to stay with a friend at university here, and the halls of residence were just round the corner from where his parents live. So when I met them, I'd seen the house before. It was like a deja vu.'

Freddy and Abe married in 1996 and have a baby son, Zack. Her parents have since bought a house in Liverpool and spend nearly every weekend here.

'Our parents are so similar. They married at the same age, and had kids. They share the same beliefs and attitudes – they even go on holiday together. The four of them look after Zack on their own – it's important that he understands that this is his family too.

'Having a baby has been a big change. I'm just finding out what I can do at the moment, but I am so lucky to have a husband and a child and a roof over my head. Abe and I spend our time taking Zack out, to the park, and to the Tate and the art galleries. Suddenly I'm getting to know the city I've lived in for ten years. I've never really lived in it before.'

प्रेम से बोलो

India

Madhu Kakar

Madhu Kakar was born in India, moving to Bradford and London before settling in Liverpool when her husband came here to study. Madhu and her husband both come from the Punjab region of northern India, which was split between India and Pakistan at the time of partition in 1947. It is a beautiful and spiritual region, but has encountered troubles since the partition.

'My husband was a qualified dentist, but his qualification was not recognised in England, so he had to do a further qualification to enable him to work as a dentist,' she explains. And so they came to Liverpool. 'I noticed how friendly it was here compared to London, but equality was pretty bad, very behind compared to cities like Bradford and Birmingham.' The Indian community is not as big in Liverpool as other cities, Madhu says, comprising only 400–500 families, but it is a powerful and professional one. 'There are more professionals here, like doctors and businessmen, whereas a lot of the communities are focussed around factories elsewhere.'

Still, nearly 30 years after Madhu first came to Liverpool, it hasn't caught up yet. 'The council started the positive action training programme in 1987–88 – before then it hardly had any black or Asian employees. But still there are not many black faces in the shops, when you go into town.'

The Hindu community – of which Madhu is the Honorary Secretary of the Cultural Organisation – is spread out across the city, rather than resident in any one area. 'Hindu families are very close-knit. They support each other, and each other's children, and are very ambitious. We want them to do better than we have done.' Like much of Liverpool, the extended family is still very evident here, particularly amongst the Hindu community: 'aunts and uncles are very important culturally. Maybe families are not as close now as they used to be, not as tight knit. Maybe even the Indian families are moving that way.'

It's not finalised yet. I'll make such a noise they have to take notice. We're supposed to be the Capital of Culture! We'll make sure there's enough hoo ha

Asked about her faith, and the strength of faith in the local community, Madhu admits that her son, who is now a neurosurgeon, doesn't share her strong faith, and that her husband doesn't practise either. 'But,' she says, 'it has kept me strong through some very difficult times. My prayers and faith and religion have given me solutions. I get peace of mind from praying when I am stressed or worried about something, and I find that it helps me think more clearly. I turn to my faith all the time – if you believe in it, and if you practise it, you will find direction – a solution to your problems, and peace. It helps you handle the situation.'

As part of this year's Year of Faith in Liverpool, Diwali – the traditional festival of light – will be celebrated at St George's

There were no white collar jobs. I didn't like it at all – I missed my friends and felt imprisoned here. It was like two different worlds

The highly-decorative Indian elephant

Hall, and the Hindu community were involved in the launch of the Year of Faith. Other than that, says Madhu, the community will see the usual Hindu festivals taking place this year.

At the moment, the community's temple on Edge Lane is still under threat from plans to widen the link from the M62 into Liverpool city centre. 'The original plan was to take four feet from the front of the building, to put the dual carriageway through. At the moment there's no parking, but people can park on the road. If the dual carriageway goes through, there'll be no parking. They either need to provide parking or take the whole building and offer us a new site,' she says. And then, with a defiant tone – although you can hear the smile in her voice: 'It's not finalised yet. I'll make such a noise they'll have to take notice. We're supposed to be the Capital of Culture! We'll make sure there's enough hoo ha!'

Madhu came to England aged 18. Her father had a good business in India, but it had hit problems, so he decided to join his brother, who was already in Bradford. 'My father worked as a bus driver when we came here, although he was later promoted to manager. There were no white collar jobs. I didn't like it at all – I missed my friends and felt imprisoned here. It was like two different worlds.' But, despite the massive culture shock, Madhu didn't let it hold her back. 'I got a job, just to get out of the house. I took a job as a sewing machinist, but I couldn't understand what anyone was saying to me. I had taken an English and Maths degree in India, but although I could read and write English, we never spoke it, and I found the Bradford accent very strong.'

Nonetheless, within a few months, and with her ear attuned to the local accent, she was interpreting for other people.

Madhu and her husband had an arranged marriage in Bradford, before moving to London and then Liverpool for his studies. Whilst her husband studied, Madhu worked as an assistant merchandiser at Littlewoods, to support him through his course.

'I was the only Asian or black person there at the time, but it caused me no problems. The problems you were more likely to face were because you were trying for a family, and from sexual discrimination.' When her husband qualified and bought his own practice, in 1977, Madhu left work to have her son.

She brought up her son at the same time as working full-time and studying part-time. She now has a Masters degree in Race Relations and Ethnic Relations, although it was more related to her work than her personal experience, she says. 'I didn't find out anything I hadn't already questioned,' but she used her experiences to get involved in community work, helping newcomers to settle in Liverpool, working as a careers adviser for the local education authority, and now as a magistrate. It's a community interest Madhu is still keen to support: 'We're seeing lots of overseas students coming to Liverpool at the moment. To support them is very important.'

Madhu radiates a great fondness for her adopted city. And, though many of her family remain in Bradford, she won't be going back there to live, not least because of the weather. 'It's too damp, it's too cold, Liverpool's much better.' But there's a much stronger conviction too: 'I have achieved so much since being in Liverpool,' she says. And now she's using those skills to help others here: 'I try to help people from all backgrounds to achieve their potential... I believe in using my skills to help others.'

JAPANESE
ORNAMENT

Japan

Frank King

Frank King, a Scouser in his mid-50s, living at the bottom of Park Lane, can claim a connection with Emperor Akihito of Japan through Frank's grandfather, Paddy Murphy.

It may sound like a Scouse shaggy dog story, but Paddy Murphy was the nickname of Frank's grandfather, Kanso Yoshida. Kanso, born in Japan in 1895, settled in Liverpool in 1938 and lived here till he died in 1973; he was a seafarer and visited Liverpool several times before deciding to make this his home.

And the connection with the Chrysanthemum Throne? It's somewhat convoluted, but Kanso was second cousin to Princess Chichibu, who was sister-in-law to Emperor Hirohito, Akihito's father.

Princess Chichibu, who was entertained at Buckingham Palace by the Queen on a royal visit in 1962, was born in England and Kanso believed 'she loved this country as I love it'.

Why Kanso left Japan and why he chose Liverpool are a mystery to Frank King, who is longing to go to Japan to research his grandfather's family. Although Frank knew Kanso all his life, it wasn't until very recently that he discovered that Kanso was his grandfather.

'My mother told me, just before she died seven years ago. Apparently my grandmother, Mabel Dingle, had been a barmaid at The Yacht in Duke Street, Kanso's local pub (he lived in Kent Gardens then). They had a bit of a fling, which resulted in my mother. My grandmother later married George Puddifer; I always knew he was my step-grandfather but never knew about Kanso being my real grandad till I was in my mid-40s.'

When he was a child, Frank used to play dominoes with Kanso and knew that the old man had a bit of a soft spot for him but, of course, didn't know why. 'When my mother told me, of course it all fell into place.'

Frank remembers Kanso as a quiet-natured man, little more than five feet tall, with something of a Scouse sense of humour. He spoke English quite well, with a bit of a Scouse accent. 'He was retired by the time I got to know him. Most of the time he was in his 'office' – otherwise known as The Yacht or The Munro, his local pubs.'

Kanso worked as a ship's fireman and donkeyman, and was in the British Navy in both World Wars. In 1917, during World War 1, his ship *Huntstrick* was torpedoed and sunk off Gibraltar, injuring Kanso badly and leaving him with a big scar down one side of his face. In World War 2 his ship was twice bombed, but Kanso escaped unhurt both times.

In May 1940, Kanso finally got his naturalisation papers, making him a British citizen. Ironic, then, that he was not interned during the war like so many other foreign nationals, or 'aliens' as they were called. It didn't save him, after Pearl Harbor in 1941, from snide remarks and some rough treatment from people who knew he was Japanese.

Says Frank: 'He was on board the Atlantic convoys going across to America, in the same boat (literally) as everyone else, his life as much at risk as any Englishman.'

In an interview in the Liverpool Echo in 1962, Kanso explained how he got his nickname: 'With a name like Kanso Yoshida it was not easy for me when I went for work to the Shipping Pool. The

The men would pretend I was enemy alien. So one day I get real mad. And I yell, 'I'm not Japanese, I'm good Englishman as any of you. If you don't like my name, I change it. Call me Paddy Murphy!'

Classical Japanese dancing, with the '…igasa', or parasol

officials and men would pretend – and sometimes they meant it, I fear – that I was enemy alien.

'So one day I get real mad at them. And I yell out, "I'm not Japanese, I'm good Englishman as any of you. If you don't like my name, then OK, I change it. Call me Paddy Murphy!" And they laughed and I am known as Paddy Murphy ever since.'

It was the war that made people suspicious, says Frank. No wonder, really, since the area of Liverpool where Kanso lived was badly bombed in the Blitz.

Frank continues: 'When I was growing up, this area was a real mixture of nationalities – Spanish, Greek, Chinese, Indian, African – and it still is. We were like a little tribe in this area; there was no racial intolerance that I ever saw.'

For almost the first 30 years of Kanso's life in Liverpool, he knew no other Japanese people; there may have been Japanese seamen in and out of the docks, but as far as Frank can discover there was no Japanese community in the city.

In 1965, though, Keinosuke Enoeda arrived in Liverpool to teach karate at the newly-formed Liverpool Karate Club. Two years earlier, Enoeda had won the all-Japan championships, so to persuade him to come to Liverpool was quite a coup for the city's sports fans.

He lived in Percy Street, in the Georgian terraces of Liverpool 8, and drove round town in a bright orange VW Beetle.

Enoeda used to admit that at first he found English food strange (he couldn't believe that we make sweet pudding from rice) as well as the British weather. But he grew to love the British people and their culture, and would say he was proud to be chief instructor to 'the best karate nation in the world', as he put it.

Enoeda and Paddy Murphy became friends, and karate expert Terry O'Neill

remembers his fierce instructor becoming quite meek in the presence of the older Kanso. 'Kanso would sometimes correct Enoeda Sensei's Japanese,' Terry laughs.

Enoeda Sensei instructed full-time at the Liverpool Red Triangle Dojo; according to Terry: 'You would have found it difficult not to be inspired by the intensity of his coaching.' Every morning at 7am in Sefton Park he would meet a small group of students – including Terry O'Neill – and train with them, showing by example that even All-Japan champions need to make training part of their daily lives.

Enoeda Sensei (Sensei is a term of respect for a teacher) became the chief karate instructor of Europe and, after his death in 2003, was awarded 9th Dan – a rare honour.

In fact, there had been a predecessor to Enoeda Sensei. Mikonosuke Kawaishi, who was born in Kyoto in 1899, studied jiu-jitsu before leaving Japan in the mid 1920s to tour the United States. In 1928 he arrived in Liverpool, where he established a jiu-jitsu club and taught the martial art. He supplemented the income from teaching by becoming a professional wrestler, using the name Matsuda. He would take on wrestlers and boxers in the ring, and on stage in the music halls. In 1931 he moved down to London where he founded the Anglo-Japanese Judo Club and taught Judo at Oxford University.

Liverpool now sees lots of Japanese visitors driven to the city by two abiding passions: football, and the Beatles. But before the Beatles hit Japan, there was the Liverpool 5. A band of friends who met on a Mersey ferry, the group was picked to be the official rock and roll outfit at the Tokyo Olympics in 1964. They were even sometimes introduced at gigs as 'the Liverpool Beatles', so it's ironic that none of them were from Merseyside.

India

Kyria Loyden

Kyria Loyden is 21. Her maternal grandparents are Indian, her paternal grandparents from Liverpool. Her mother was brought up in Hong Kong, her dad is a professional footballer from Liverpool who has played professionally all over the world. She lives in Liverpool with her parents. Her grandparents are just around the corner...

'When I was younger we visited the places my family has come from. India was such a big culture shock, I really wasn't expecting it at all. It's still so Third World – I was expecting it to be more commercial, especially Delhi, because it's a capital city. There are so many beggars and homeless people, so much traffic on the roads, and pollution and crowds. I remember going to the Taj Mahal and it was so beautiful, but just outside there were mud huts, and there was a body on the floor – a dead man. People were just stepping over him. I was really shocked... It's just so different – standing there, trying to have a bath or a shower, with just a bucket. I mean, it's supposed to be the capital.'

Emigration from India to Hong Kong started in the mid 19th century when both were British colonies. The British took Muslim soldiers with them to Hong Kong, and merchants followed in their wake. Both Hindus and Sikhs now number amongst Hong Kong's thriving Indian community; 12,000 Hindus now live in Hong Kong, but they make up a full 10% of the lucrative garment industry in the territory.

The oldest shrine in Hong Kong is at Happy Valley – the Hindu community was allocated land in a cemetary there, along with each different Hong Kong community. But the administrator clearly didn't realise that the Hindus cremate rather than bury their dead, and had no need for a cemetary. So in a densely populated area – with phenomenal land values – the Hindu community used the land to build their temple.

> They kept their blossoming relationship a secret. She was from a strict Indian family; he was white, 12 years older, and a footballer

Kyria's grandparents moved to Hong Kong from India, looking for a better standard of living. They had married on Valentine's Day 1958 – although, as Hindus, they didn't celebrate the festival – and moved to Hong Kong, where Kyria's mother Nita was born. Some of their relatives had already moved to Hong Kong, where there was – and still is – a thriving Indian community. Kyria says: 'It was a very close-knit community – my mum and all her friends were in it and everyone knew each other. They'd only go out with other Indians, and if one of them was seen out unchaperoned with someone who wasn't – everyone would know about it. They just transplanted their culture there.'

Some of the community remains very tight-knit: 'I've got an auntie in Hong Kong who's travelled very widely and will mix with anyone, but her husband – who

He turned around and said that I shouldn't have a go at him, because 'we're on the same side, you and me, against these white people'

is also Indian – likes to stay with his Indian friends and wants his children brought up like that too. The way of life is just so different.'

Kyria's family visited Hong Kong every year during the summer holidays to visit her grandparents and it's somewhere that she'd consider living in the future. 'Hong Kong's just busy, 24/7. It's futuristic and you've got everything there you need. It's so vibrant, and I absolutely love it. You feel so safe, whatever time of night it is there are crowds and people, and no crime. Well, not in the same way... I'd love to live there. I'd like to go abroad – England's not for me.'

Kyria's mother Nita met her father Eddie – who comes from Seaforth – in Hong Kong, where he was playing professional football. She would visit a cafe for her tea breaks and the footballers congregated there for breakfast after morning training. They kept their blossoming relationship a secret – she was from a strict Indian family; he was white, 12 years older, and a footballer. Kyria says: 'Mum's family wanted her to have an arranged marriage – to marry a typical Indian. But someone saw her out with my dad and everything came out one night in a horrible argument.'

Shortly after, Eddie's contract ended with his Hong Kong club, and with it went his accommodation. He was offered a new contract in New Zealand, but – hearing of family health problems – had to return to England suddenly. 'His going away gave mum some time to decide which avenue she was going to follow, but she followed her heart and followed my dad. Hong Kong wasn't enough any more. I can't believe it – she was only 19

The mausoleum of the mughal Empress Mumtaz Mahal – or Taj Mahal
Agra, India

or 20 when she left, and all she knew was life in Hong Kong and Asia. She took a flight to India, and from there made her way to England. My dad was waiting at Heathrow, but she managed to miss her flight, so he had to sit there, waiting all night, not knowing whether she was going to come or not.'

Unlike the resistance that Nita faced, Eddie didn't experience the same sort of objections to his relationship in Hong Kong: 'Prejudice wasn't a problem in Hong Kong – lots of his team mates had Chinese girlfriends. But when they came to England, it wasn't the done thing; it was very hard for them.'

It's something that Kyria feels hasn't really changed in Liverpool. 'I think it's a joke that this is going to be Capital of Culture. It's just not race-friendly. I've had so much abuse – at school, in the street – that I can't imagine what it was like for my mum when she came here. It's not just white people – a black man stopped me at Waterloo station one day and asked me if I was off to the Taj Mahal restaurant, assuming that my family owned it. I had a right go at him – just because I'm half Asian doesn't mean that I was going to the curry house. He turned around and said that I shouldn't have a go at him, because "we're on the same side, you and me, against these white people." My dad, who is white, was picking me up. I just wished he'd get out of the car at that moment.

'I also get comments from Asian lads, especially in Manchester, when I'm out with my boyfriend, who's white. I can understand why people stick to their own. It's only a small percentage of people that cause problems, but it's why communities stick together. I think that's so sad.'

After settling in Liverpool together, Kyria's parents had a quiet wedding.

Things settled down once they had married, particularly when they had their first child. 'It was a turning point, and when my sister was born my grandparents from Hong Kong came to visit for the first time.' It was, she says, a question of different expectations: 'It's accepted more now – it wasn't then. It's funny, after the marriage, how things changed. How you come to rely on the people you never thought you would.'

The family have all come together again now. Eight years ago Kyria's grandparents emigrated to Liverpool from Hong Kong. Her grandfather died several years ago, but her grandmother still lives with the rest of the family, visits the Hindu temple on Edge Lane and has settled into the local community.

'They came here and decided they wanted to be here for the rest of their lives. They already had family here, which made things easier. My dad would take my grandad out for a walk in his wheelchair and, when my grandad died, my grandmother got a job in a charity shop. She's really settled. There was just too much hustle and bustle for them in Hong Kong. Too many crowds and not much green – it's quieter here. Hong Kong is a young person's place, and it's hard to survive there on a pension.'

The two sets of grandparents became friends, creating a family with Indian, Scouse and Hong Kong roots. 'Things change... my grandparents weren't expecting a footballer – they thought they were scoundrels. But my grandfather came to have so much respect for my father. My mum and dad have been married for 24 years now and have never looked back. My sister and I live in the same house that my mother arrived in 25 years ago. Two very diverse cultures have settled and become one big family in Liverpool.'

DIY

Ireland

Mary Maxwell

Mary Maxwell's roots are Irish. Her family came to Liverpool variously from Wexford, Cork, Dublin and Northern Ireland. Her great-grandparents arrived here during the Great Hunger. Whilst the family has retained strong Irish and Liverpudlian roots, it's also a family that has spread out across the world.

'My maternal great-grandparents are Irish, although they didn't meet until they came to Liverpool. My mother's grandfather was from Wexford and his wife was from County Mayo. They lived on Park Road and settled in the same court, which would have been a place of great poverty, with a shared toilet between all residents of the court.'

Mary's grandmother, Mary Howard, was one of their children. 'They also had identical twin sons and three or four daughters. The twins – Matthew and Michael – joined the navy at 21 and both died on the same day, both of a fever, on completely different sides of the world.'

Mary Howard lived in the Toxteth area all her life, and worked on Liverpool's docks, loading bails of paper onto horse-drawn wagons for George Henry Lee.

Mary Maxwell has an early photo of her grandmother with three of her children, taken around 1904. Mary Howard married an Irishman from Dublin called James. He managed a maypole shop and together they had six children, including Mary's mother, Elizabeth, her aunt, Rose – who served in France during World War 1 aged just 12 or 13 – and her uncle, Michael, who was killed in the Dardanelles as a boy soldier in 1916.

I did the trip in reverse with my mother's sister. I took a cargo ship from Birkenhead, her coffin was in a hearse. It was really quite emotional, knowing that my family came down the Mersey on the cattle ships, and I was taking them back

The Dardanelles was a key World War 1 battle, as British forces tried to open up the Dardanelles Straight, which protects Istanbul from the Mediterranean. The heavily mined stretch of water caused huge loss of life, with the Allied forces – including soldiers from Australia and New Zealand – losing more than 700 men by the time of its retreat.

'I traced the landing field where my Uncle Mike was killed and his name is on a cenotaph in Basrah. I was astounded, whilst watching the news recently, to see the British soldiers come across this old First World War memorial.'

Mary's aunt, Rose Howard, married a man called George Fox. He worked on the White Star liners, sailing out of Liverpool to America and Canada, but was killed when a drunken passenger hit him round the head with a spanner. The White Star Line paid for his daughter, May, to travel to Montreal to see his grave (the ship was on its way to Montreal when he died) – she met an American woman en route who invited her to stay in New York. May met and married her

The Emerald Isle: Glendove
Ireland

son, and to this day a whole branch of the family lives in and around Long Island.

'The American side of the family has a very strong connection with Liverpool,' says Mary, 'but also a strong one with Ireland. They're torn between the two.'

Wherever in the world Mary's family are now, their Irish connections remain important. 'Irishness stands out in people, all over the world,' she says. 'It's very much a stamp. If you hold an Irish passport you'll be welcome anywhere in the world. The Irish have never colonised anyone,' she laughs.

Mary's father was also Irish – his mother brought her 14 children to Liverpool from Cork when her father was just three, and all of the children were brought up here. He was an engineer at Cammell Laird and closely escaped death when the Thetis sank in June 1939.

It was the first naval submarine built on Merseyside and sank on its first dive. 'He'd had an argument with my mother and got drunk,' she says. 'He missed the trial. The Thetis sank.' Ninety-nine people died on board the submarine as it sank into the mud of Liverpool Bay.

Mary's father – she is one of his 10 children – was one of the lucky ones that day but, after he volunteered for the Navy in 1943, he was killed when a kamikaze pilot hit his aircraft carrier at Bombay.

Mary's husband's roots are Northern Irish. They have a daughter and three sons. Whilst her sons remain in Liverpool, the story has come full circle – Mary's daughter now has Irish nationality, through her own husband. 'They met in Liverpool, but have moved back across the Irish Sea to live in Dublin.'

It's interesting – with Liverpool's Capital of Culture year coming up in 2008 – to compare the city with Dublin, which was European City of Culture in 1991. 'My daughter wasn't there when Dublin was

City of Culture, but it did do very well with the Celtic Tiger. It'll be interesting to see what happens to Liverpool, what impact it has here' she says.

'She actually stood for the Irish Parliament after leading a campaign about mobile phone masts near schools. She did so well, but in the end she didn't want to be a politician. They call her "the English woman" there and she is still very English in many ways.'

Clearly the Irish cultural roots go deep. 'My father was one of 14, and amongst them there were two priests, two nuns, a headmaster and a doctor. One of the priests was a Gaelic lecturer, and taught other priests in his own language. And now my grandson has to learn Irish as part of his certificate.' Mary too has studied Irish and took a Masters degree in Irish Studies when she retired. 'I did my dissertation on the impact of land confiscation in the late 17th century, and studied ancient Irish law – which was actually very fair, especially for women – so I know something of where my ancestors came from.

'Liverpool is the only university in the UK to have an Irish Studies department.

'I love Ireland and try to get over as much as I can. The culture's lovely – the fiddlers, the singers, the dancing. It's very sad that the Irish Centre in Liverpool's gone. People do tend to revert to their roots, especially as they get older.'

As is often the case in life, events go in cycles. Mary felt that Ireland was the right place to take her aunt back to when she died. 'I did the trip in reverse with my mother's sister. I took a cargo ship from Birkenhead, her coffin was in a hearse. It was really quite emotional, knowing that my family came down the Mersey on the cattle ships and I was taking them back.'

Greece

Athanassios Migos

His name means 'one blessed with immortality', and he describes himself as Hellenic. And he was born in Larisa, which is no more than a thunderbolt's cast from Mount Olympus. So by rights, he could be a Greek god. But Athanassios Migos would not be content with a restrictive menu, even nectar and ambrosia served up by a goddess.

One of the abiding memories he has of his first year in England is the relentless offerings of fish and chips every Friday, and sausages, fried bread and brown sauce every Saturday. 'Every Saturday,' he stresses. 'For eight months.'

It is a far cry from the enterprise that has got Athanassios into the latest guide to North West Fine Foods. He has brought the traditional Greek skills of spit roasting to the English at home. 'Anything from a partridge to an ox,' he says. Don't think 'barbecue'; a traditional spit roast takes half a day to prepare, a day to roast, and half a day to clear up. It's a serious business, and the Migos enterprise is taking a highly professional approach to the venture, with ten staff trained so far.

Athanassios learned from his Epirot grandfather, in the mountain villages of north west Greece. 'My grandfather used to travel around the villages spit roasting meat for saints' day celebrations every year, and I'd go with him to help. He had a flock of sheep and goats and would take two or three animals to each festival, which might be a day's walk, and roast them for the village. People would come from miles around – it was a huge thing.'

Athanassios and his younger brother Spiros were born in Larisa, 'the Birmingham of Greece,' as he puts it, but until he was 14, the family would spend two or three months each summer in Epiros with his grandparents. 'It was a very self-sufficient life they lived. No electricity, water had to be fetched from the stream, you lived off what you could produce from the land and from your flocks.'

Later the family went to the sea for the summer, and in 1974 they built a house in Stomion, on the slopes of Mount Ossa, on the Aegean coast, where the River Pinios reaches the sea.

Recently, Athanassios has bought two ruined houses in the historic village of Ambelakia (also on Ossa), where the world's first ever co-operative society was set up at the end of the 18th century, to dye cotton yarn and sell it across Europe.

He loves the history of it. 'Archaeology – the way people lived, their stories – that was my first love. But I could always draw well, so it seemed that architecture was a good choice.'

He is now a lecturer in architecture at Liverpool John Moores University.

'Actually,' he adds with a laugh, 'I had a little business in the last two years of high school: because my technical drawing was good, other students would come to me to draw for them, for fifty drachmas a time. I had to make variations on each copy, of course, or else the teacher would spot the fraud. What made me mad was that the copies got them better marks than my originals got me! Still, the fifty drachmas were some compensation.'

The fact that Athanassios was at school at all was a matter of great pride to his family. Neither of his parents could read or write. 'My father went to school in September 1940, and then the war began, and that was the end of that. My mother had no education; she looked after the

I was so shy; the only company I had was the landlady's cat. I realised that if I carried on this way, I was going to be an unhappy man

family's flock, and her little brother and sister. That was the way of it for girls at that time. If my mother had gone to school she would have been prime minister of Greece – she was a very capable woman,' he says with pride.

'My father was a travelling tinker – in its literal sense. People had bronze pots to eat from, but since bronze is poisonous, they needed to be lined with tin. My father travelled round Greece, tinning pots.'

Later he became a dowry seller, marketing fabrics, linen, tablecloths and so on to girls collecting their trousseau.

'My parents sent me to the foreign school to learn English, and in the mid 1970s I decided I didn't want to go to a Greek university. To be a student in Greece meant being a political animal – this was not long after the Colonels' junta had ended – and that was not for me.'

The first thought was Italy, but a contact of his father's said that an Italian degree was a waste of effort and that Athanassios, aged 17, should go to America or England. America was too far and too expensive, so England it was. He went to the British Council in Salonica to look for information on colleges in England, but got caught by a con man who gave him a leaflet for the Centre for Business and Scientific Studies in London. 'He took 25,000 drachmas from me – a month's wages for my father.

'Well, when I got to London I searched this place out. It was a rented house by Woolwich market; there was a bingo hall on the ground floor, and upstairs was the class, with 23 Greeks and two Turks.'

He stuck it for a month.

He had at least found digs – the Saturday sausage place. 'It was a zoo: 25

Classical Greece meets commercial Greece: the harbour on the island of Symi

animals in the house,' he says.

On his first weekend in London, he got all dressed up for a night on the town, and headed for downtown Bexley Heath. The streets so full of life in the day were, after 6pm, a desert. 'I couldn't believe it. What a culture shock.'

The next attempt at an English education was better. After a trip back home, Athanassios headed for the Cheltenham College of Technology, where he had two marvellous years doing A levels. His landlady was Scouse, and filled his head with tales of an amazing city, friendly people, their sense of humour. He was sold, and applied for a place at Liverpool University.

When he arrived at Rathbone hall of residence, he looked out of the window, and across the road he could see the street sign Penny Lane. 'That was it, I was home,' he says. Without a grant, he had to fund himself through university, which meant working at night. 'I think I worked in every Greek restaurant in the city, and a few others. No social life, of course.'

He would live on food he brought home from the restaurants that would otherwise have been thrown away, but other students discovered this stash of good eatables and would raid his fridge. 'I would get home at 1am or 2am and find them lined up waiting for me and my bags of kebabs, or whatever. I was feeding half of Rathbone Hall,' he laughed.

Athanassios progressed from kitchen porter up to the glorified position of head waiter. 'I paid my university fees in instalments, and in cash. And I mean I was in the administrator's office counting out the pennies.' Then his brother Spiros arrived to do an HND at Liverpool Poly. Spiros got a job at the kebab house, and the Migos brothers ended up being hired as Greek dancers. 'We got £15 each for 11 minutes dancing, which kept us going for the whole week – rent, food, fees, the lot.'

Athanassios got his degree, then got a job with local architects Kingham Knight, where he worked on the sewage treatment works at Sandon Dock. He is still upset that his design for a glass dome was scratched. '£40 million and they begrudged me £200,000 for a glass dome which would have been unique in the world,' he growls.

After a year working for architects in Zurich, it was back here for a Master's degree at York, another stint at Kingham Knight, a PhD, then in 1989 the teaching job at JMU.

Now with his wife Trisha and three children he is thoroughly rooted in Liverpool, and the family's catering business – Spit Roasts Unlimited – is, to coin a phrase, consuming him.

What about the Greek community in Liverpool? Athanassios points out that there are the Greek Greeks, and the Greek Cypriots who, he says, 'have anti-Greek sentiment built into their genes.' There is little trace of the wealthy 19th century Greek merchants who came to Liverpool, like shipowner George Papayannis, or the Ralli family (remembered in the name of Ralli House) who were involved in the cotton trade. 'The Greek poet Cafavy, who was also in the cotton trade, came here,' says Athanassios. Now there are lots of Greek Greeks in Liverpool again – university students.

Athanassios looks back to two major decisions early in his life. The second was to stay here when his father became ill and couldn't send him any more money. The first, made the first week in London, changed his life. 'I was so shy; the only company I had was the landlady's cat. I realised that if I carried on this way, I was going to be an unhappy man. So I decided to live life to the full, and I changed. I just stopped being shy,' he laughed.

ONGOMANIA
TEL.
264
D IN ONE CITY ★ LIVERPOOL 20
CONGOMANIA
LIVERPOOL
BAR DEMILLE
The Liverpool Olympia

Democratic Republic of Congo

Emmanuel Muanda

Imagine being forced to abandon your whole life to escape being killed by your own countrymen. Imagine leaving the country you love, travelling many thousands of miles north into the freezing winter of Europe, only to be stopped from reaching friends who were going to help you begin again. With no intention of spending more time in Britain than it took to get a connecting flight to Romania, Emmanuel Muanda was collared by the British immigration authorities.

He claimed political asylum, and the refugee arrival project found him somewhere to stay in London while his future was being decided for him.

After two days in a London hotel – which was not exactly Claridge's – Emmanuel Muanda was packed off to Liverpool, even though he had been trying to get to his friends in Bucharest. But having been stopped by the immigration authorities at Heathrow Airport when he was trying to get the connecting flight, he found he had little choice in the matter.

'Liverpool was for me the city of my dreams since my childhood, but the news and myths I heard during my two days in London were not encouraging,' he says.

So without much alternative, 'I accepted to come to Liverpool... ouf!'

It was a culture shock.

Liverpool is a very long way from his homeland, the third largest country in Africa – the Democratic Republic of Congo. Within a few days Emmanuel had gone from the equatorial heat of West Africa to the cold greyness of Liverpool in the pre-Christmas rush.

'On the street there was nobody to speak to, and worse was the language barrier, isolation and ignorance,' he says.

It was a grim future, but there was no chance of going back to Africa, so Emmanuel did the only thing he could.

'I decided to fight these problems by forgetting my past and getting to know Liverpool.

'I managed to learn some English, and took on the responsibility for helping others in similar situations, by establishing a community welcome project. This does a lot of work for newly arrived refugees and the city's Congolese community.'

Emmanuel became a refugee in 1998 when he was accused of collaborating with the enemy. Along with some 300,000 others, Emmanuel had to flee a war spawned by rebels backed by Uganda and Rwanda – but this was the latest in a long series of ethnic conflict and civil war which have done such massive damage to the country. Since 1998, GDP has plummeted; debt has soared, and through disease, war and famine, some 3.5 million Congolese have died.

Back in 1965, five years after DR Congo won independence from Belgium, the country's first prime minister was assassinated and Joseph Mobutu seized power and renamed the country Zaire. Over the next 37 years the dictator built a personal fortune of an estimated $5 billion from his country's natural riches, when the average annual income in Zaire was $210.

In March 1997, rebel leader Laurent Kabila – who had tried unsuccessfully to topple Mobutu in the mid 1960s – captured Kisangani; by May Mobutu had been ousted from power; Kabila took control and renamed the country DR Congo. Four months later Mobutu died, in Morocco, of cancer. Kabila lasted less than three years before being assassinated; his

Liverpool was for me the city of my dreams since my childhood, but the news and myths I heard in London were not encouraging.... ouf!

son Joseph Kabila became head of state, promising free elections in 2006 and working with UN support to bring peace and stability to his country.

Mobutu had left Zaire bankrupt and blood-stained. Garrick Utley, a correspondent for CNN, reported from Kinshasa in 1997, when President Mobutu was still in power at the end of his 37-year reign. Utley said: 'Imagine being mugged as you walk down a street. But you can't go to the authorities for protection because, chances are, they are the muggers. Now imagine an entire country of 45 million people being mugged by their own leader.

'Unfortunately there is nothing imaginary about this, if you are in Zaire.'

In some ways, nothing much has changed in 100 years. In 1904 a report by the British Consul in Congo, Roger Casement, provoked a scandal that rocked Europe and the USA. And this was due to a campaign waged by a young Liverpool shipping clerk.

Edmund Morel was born in Paris in 1873, but when his father died four years later, his mother took the boy back to England. Morel went to school in Sussex, and at the age of 18 he got a clerical job in Liverpool with the shipping company Elder Dempster, which mainly served the ports of West Africa, and was involved in Congo's rich rubber trade.

A committed Quaker, Morel became deeply concerned about the damage that he believed British trade was doing to African culture, especially the rubber trade in Congo. On trips to Antwerp for his employers, Morel was supervising the loading and unloading of ships, and noticed that although they were coming back from Africa with holds full of rubber

Pirogues – or dug-out canoes – on the Congo river
Democratic Republic of Congo (formerly Zaire)

and ivory, they had gone out with cargoes of arms and non-trading goods. With nothing to trade, how were the merchants getting hold of such profitable cargoes? The answer, inevitably, was slavery, slaughter and atrocity.

'I had stumbled on a secret society of murderers with a king for a partner,' Morel wrote later.

It turned out that Leopold II, king of the Belgians, had grabbed Congo as his own personal colony in 1884, had sent troops out there and had created a forced labour camp on a massive scale. The rainforests of Congo were full of rubber – which in 1890, became the new gold. Tapping wild rubber was difficult, so Leopold's agents used brutal force to get the Congolese to collect the stuff. Women would be abducted and kept in chains to force their husbands to gather rubber; boys would have their hands cut off and other mutilations. If villages resisted Leopold's wishes, his Force Publique would destroy the villages and kill the people; for proof, officers demanded to see the amputated right hand of every corpse.

Morel wrote a series of articles on the Congo Scandal in 1900, and after having to resign from Elder Dempster, became a full-time journalist, and set up the Congo Reform Association in 1904. He took a leading role in several other campaigning bodies, and recruited support from the likes of Arthur Conan Doyle, Mark Twain, and Joseph Conrad (who wrote *Heart of Darkness* having seen the atrocities for himself). Eventually the British government sent Casement to investigate, and the report was so shocking that the original was never published. Leopold II, however, was forced in 1908 to sell his colony to the Belgian government (at vast cost) and the whole shameful horror was swept under the carpet.

Elder Dempster, Morel's employer, was

run by the man who founded Liverpool's pioneering School of Tropical Medicine, Sir Alfred Lewis Jones, one of the city's great philanthropists. The School – now part of the University of Liverpool – was founded in 1898, the year that Morel began his campaign, and in the next 15 years despatched 32 expeditions to the heart of Africa to research disease.

The second prize for medicine ever to be awarded by the Nobel Foundation, in 1902, went to the School's professor Ronald Ross. Ross had joined the School in 1899 and was immediately sent to West Africa, where he found that the Anophiles mosquito was the means by which the malaria parasite is transmitted.

A century later, malaria is still undefeated, with four million new cases registered in DR Congo in 2003; it is the leading cause of infant mortality in the country.

The School of Tropical Medicine's 12th expedition, in 1904, included the Wirral-born pathologist Joseph Everett Dutton who was researching what the explorer David Livingstone called human tick disease. Dutton, during a post mortem, managed to infect himself with the same disease, and died in February 1905. He is buried in Kosongo, Congo, and has the fatal bug named after him: *Borrelia duttonii*. Some legacy.

Emmanuel Muanda may not be in a position to change the course of his homeland's history, but he is committed to his adopted home. Now running Congomania, a business set up to support the Congolese Association of Liverpool, he wants to help change the image of the city with projects linked to the Capital of Culture. 'I never stop telling people to move to Liverpool or invest in the opportunities that Capital of Culture will bring.

'I have a lot to share with people about this amazing city,' he says.

Barbados

Rudolph Murray

In the greatest of seafaring traditions, Rudolph Murray came to Liverpool from Barbados. He joined the merchant navy aged 18, in 1952, and was promptly off to sea with the Harrison Line, taking cargo first to Falmouth and London, before arriving in Liverpool.

Like most sailors he spent months at sea, on epic voyages that took the cargo ships from Barbados and on to South Africa and South America – via England – on their three-month round trips.

You can still see the headquarters of the Harrison Shipping Line opposite the Liver Building. The white Liver Bird above the entrance is an indication of the company's significance to the city of Liverpool; known as the 'third Liver Bird', in fact it is older than its larger green cousins on top of the Liver Building.

The Harrison Line was formed in Liverpool in 1853; originally it imported brandy from France, but gradually acquired more and more steamships and traded predominantly with the Caribbean, Latin America, South and East Africa. The journey from Barbados to the UK alone took three weeks: 'We brought sugar to Liverpool and would sail into the Huskisson and Albert Docks, via Canary Wharf and Burfleet' says Rudolph. 'Then, on the return leg, we'd take electrical items and clothing back.'

Liverpool's connections with Barbados go back for centuries. The islands offered a haven for people fleeing the country in the aftermath of the war, whether from political or religious persecution. In the 1640s Liverpool's ships were trading there; the English Civil War had diverted money and attention away from Liverpool's trading partners and the West Indies filled that gap. Notoriously, at the close of the 17th century, Liverpool merchants learned from other cities that money was to be made in human cargo: Liverpool's first recorded slaver, the *Liverpool Merchant*, sold her cargo of 220 West Africans in Barbados in 1700.

The long history of trade links with Barbados contributed to the establishment of one of the country's oldest black communities here. John Archer – who became Britain's first black mayor in 1913 – was the Liverpool-born son of a Barbadian ship's steward. On taking his new role, he famously declared: 'I am the son of a man born in the West Indian islands. I was born in the city of Liverpool. My mother was an Irish woman. My election tonight marks a new era; you have made history.' His portrait hangs in Liverpool town hall.

It wasn't Rudolph's original intention to stay in Liverpool. 'I thought I'd earn some money and go back, but I've got no regrets,' he says.

That's where fate stepped in. 'We went out in every port and in Liverpool everybody went to the Grafton when the ship came in: Thursdays, Fridays, Saturday nights.' And that's where he met his wife Marie, who was born in Liverpool but came from another seafaring family – her Portuguese father was chief engineer on the Larrinaga Line.

Rudolph and Marie married in 1956 and settled in Liverpool when Marie decided she didn't fancy life in a hot climate. Like many sailors in Liverpool, Rudolph worked as a taxi driver and a bus driver, unable to find work here as an engineer.

His first home was on Stanhope Street, with his in-laws, and he talks warmly

Religion is much more popular in the States. My theory is that in England there is a pub on every corner, in the States it's a church

The windward side of the West Indies
Newcastle, Barbados

about Liverpool in his soft Caribbean accent. 'I feel part of the community here. I've always been one for going along with the crowd. I don't like a lonely life.'

His memories of Liverpool are fond, but perhaps one of the most memorable is the night the roof collapsed at the St James cinema. 'It was 1957 or 1958 and I'd gone to the cinema with my wife to watch a film. The roof just fell in! I can't even remember what the film was now, but it was a love story, with Humphrey Bogart. Nobody was hurt, but everybody just ran for their lives. Everyone was panicking, but we laughed after. Can you imagine that happening now? There'd be all kinds of compensation.'

Rudolph and Marie have a son and a daughter, seven grandchildren, and a great grandson, who's a bit of a handful according to his great-grandad. 'The kids like Barbados. They know the culture, they like the fresh meals, and the sea, but Liverpool's their home.' More recently, Rudolph and Marie have thought of retiring to Barbados, where money goes further. But now they have the luxury of being able to go backwards and forwards, escaping the worst of the heat.

'Barbados is only a small colony, and most people think about leaving to make a bob or two, but I was thinking of going back and building somewhere. I've still got family in Barbados, but lots in America and Canada too, including a sister in New York.' Scattered as his family is, they've all been over to visit Liverpool. 'The American bunch always think it's quieter than the US. It's a quieter nation, more obedient. Although I think we're starting to go the other way now!'

Rudolph spends a lot of time in the States as a Bishop with the Apostolic Episcopal church – a role he's had since 1994. 'I've always been religious. I sang in a choir when I was a kid and I served on

the altar in the Roman Catholic church. I even wanted to be a priest when I was younger, but there weren't opportunities for black priests in the Catholic church at the time. In Barbados, all the priests were white – that's why I moved to the Episcopal church. But there's always some controversy; whether it's black priests, or women priests. I just go for the Lord.'

Rudolph carries out weddings, christenings and burials (he even led part of the service at his sister's funeral) in his role as Bishop, although all services need to be formalised by a registrar. His Liverpool church was on Earle Road in Kensington, but the congregation slowly died out and the church has since closed. 'Now I travel a lot more, to London and to America,' he says. 'Religion is much more popular in the States. My theory is that in England there is a pub on every corner, in the States it's a church. I think the black community there has faced so much oppression and segregation they needed something to turn to to keep them stable.'

And what about the Portuguese influence in the Murray home? 'The community's not very big here. We do eat Portuguese food, like paella. And sometimes we go to the cafe in town, which always makes my wife come home and cook something Portuguese!'

The Caribbean, Portuguese and English influences have all mixed in the Murray home: 'I like the dancing, the steel bands, playing dominoes, cricket and golf,' says Rudolph. 'But it's a happy medium. Like anywhere, things have changed, and Liverpool has changed so much since I first came here. I enjoyed the strong sense of community – everyone used to leave their front door open. The younger generation is different, but this is my home.'

Philippines

Teresa O'Brien

Teresa Francesca O'Brien was born in Liverpool, but her family's roots are in Manila, in the Philippines. Her father and her mother's grandfather were seafarers who came to Liverpool on ships from the East.

Liverpool's Filipino community was a significant one, predominantly made up of sailors – the Philippines is a former Spanish colony and the Spanish seafarers were keen to open up fast trade routes between their colonies and Europe.

Although the English captured Manila from the Spanish, and ruled the city for two years between 1762 and 1764, it seems that few Filipinos had the chance to travel to England. Whilst Indian and Chinese sailers were already serving on board British ships, fierce rivalry between the Spanish and the English forbade Filipinos from joining crews on English boats – the Seven Years War was raging in Europe, and Filipinos were classified as Spanish citizens. It wasn't until the Treaty of Paris ended the war in 1763 that control of Manila was handed back to the Spanish.

Teresa's great-grandfather, Matthew Ignacio, came to Liverpool from Manila in 1840. He became a boarding house keeper in Liverpool and is listed here in the 1881 census.

The Filipino community had become well established in the boarding houses on Hurst Street and Frederick Street, close to Kings Dock, where Spaniards and Filipinos ran boarding houses catering for people from their own countries. Little of the area is recognisable today, however – its proximity to the docks made it a target for bombs during the war and is almost unrecognisable today, with new developments filling the gaps left by the Blitz.

Juan Saron, Teresa's father, also came to Liverpool from the Philippines, marrying her mother Mary Ann Rapole here in 1913. Juan and Mary Ann were married at St Peter's Roman Catholic church on Seel Street, through which the family were later able to begin tracing their history.

Juan was a seaman, employed by the Spanish Larrinaga Shipping Line, which was founded here in 1862 by Spaniards living in Liverpool.

Larrinaga Line ships can be traced back as far as 1773 in Bilbao, Spain, but the company was based in Liverpool from the 1860s onwards. The completion of the Suez Canal in 1869 opened up trade routes to the East and the Larrinaga Line moved away from its traditional sailing ships to new, faster steam ships, which could travel up and down the canal.

Regular services between Europe and Asia only started with the opening of the Suez, and general cargoes, as well as mail, were regularly sent by ship after that. It was the Basque Trading Company that took full advantage of the new canal, opening up the shipping lines between Liverpool, Cadiz in Spain, and Manila.

The seamen often met Liverpool girls

In the last few years there has been a new influx of Filipinos into Liverpool, this time thanks to the National Health Service

Her great-grandfather, Matthew Ignacio, came to Liverpool from Manila the same year 1840 that Samuel Cunard began his packet boat sailings to America

Tourists and outrigger canoes line White Sun beach
Boracay Island, Panay, the Philippines

while they were staying here, usually at the boarding houses which they stayed in whilst in Liverpool. Juan Saron married Mary Ann, whom he met in Liverpool. She was Liverpool-born (her grandfather, Matthew Ignacio, had come to Liverpool from Manila the same year – 1840 – that Samuel Cunard began his packet boat sailings from Liverpool to America).

Teresa is one of their seven children; all her brothers, like their ancestors, became seamen, but as the maritime trade links declined, they worked for the merchant navy rather than the old shipping lines that had originally brought their family to Liverpool.

Her father, Juan, died when she was three, and the family moved away from the Filipino community where she was brought up, at Shaw's Alley, by the King's Dock. Although Teresa's older brothers and sisters remember their Filipino father, her knowledge of him comes mostly from the stories she was told as a child.

Deborah, Teresa's daughter, and her brother began tracing the family's history when St Peter's church in Seel Street closed down and its records were transferred to microfilm. She says: 'It's quite hard tracking people down from that period – there weren't a lot of records then. I'm not even sure if my grandad was nationalised British – I don't think many people were at the time. He was never registered as living here – the only clues we could find were some photographs and the information on my mother's birth certificate. But finally we spotted my mother's maiden name, Saron, and were able to trace our family all the way back to the 1860s.'

After Juan's death, Teresa's family gradually moved away from their roots in the dockside Filipino community and eventually moved to a new house in

Huyton, where they were one of the only Filipino families.

Teresa and her mother would go back to Seel Street to see Father Primavesi, the priest who had married Mary Ann and Juan at St Peter's; but the change in the patterns of world trade meant that fewer Filipino sailors came to Liverpool to stay, and by the end of the 20th century, the community's historic links with the dock had virtually disappeared.

In the last few years, however, there has been a new influx of Filipinos into Liverpool, this time thanks to the National Health Service.

Teresa's daughter Deborah is a nurse at Whiston hospital, which is building a growing Filipino community. 'There are about 300 Filipino nurses at Whiston now: it's a very strong community there. They're very religious – they're Catholics – and when they celebrate events like christenings they invite everyone over.

'Whenever they see Deborah they ask her if she's got Filipino blood – they can really see it in her – and they think she has quite a lot of Filipino traits. But they don't understand why Deborah's not married yet with children, as they can be quite old-fashioned and traditional.

'It's not just female nurses that have come over though, there are lots of men too, and many of them have married since they've been in Liverpool. But in all the time Deborah has been there – which is about four years – only one girl has married an English husband.'

Teresa has never been back to the Philippines to get a glimpse of her family's culture and history, but Deborah plans to make the trip for her honeymoon: 'She would love to go and see what it's really all like. It's just a great thought for her to be able to go back to her roots.'

Wales

Barry Owen

Liverpool was, for some time, so Welsh that the city hosted six National Eisteddfod, between 1840 and 1929; at the start of the 20th century, Liverpool had a larger Welsh speaking population than Cardiff or Swansea.

There were several Welsh language local newspapers; even today the Liverpool Daily Post has its Welsh edition, sold throughout North Wales, and carrying the red dragon on the masthead.

From Liverpool's hills the view is across the Wirral to the Clwydian mountains and, from the top of tall buildings, over to Llandudno's Great Orme and even, on clear days, to Snowdon itself.

The Welsh have been coming to Liverpool for well over 1,000 years – names like Walton and Wallasey point to ancient settlements; they have played leading roles in the city's history ever since. Liverpool's mayor from 1503 to 1515, for instance, was one Dafydd ap Gruffydd.

Barry Owen is a product of Liverpool Welsh; three of his grandparents were Welsh (his mother's mother was Liverpool Irish) and his father was a Welsh speaker.

In the 1860s, the family were tenant sheep farmers at Llanfachreth, near Dolgellau: 'My grandfather married a Welsh girl, of course, and came to Liverpool where he became a warehouse manager.

'My father was born in 1902 into a very Welsh household; they lived in Anfield Road, but his father sent him back to Dolgellau at the age of about 10 to get a proper Welsh education, and to learn the discipline of Welsh Methodists. Religion and education were the lynchpins of his life; my father was a lifelong subscribing member of the Welsh-speaking Douglas Road Methodist Church.

'At the age of 17 my father got a job with the Midland Bank in Liverpool and ended up as a manager. He would look after the Welsh chaps at the bank, so at his branch to be Welsh was a great bonus if you were looking for promotion.'

Since Barry's mother was Irish, he didn't grow up speaking Welsh as his father had done. 'I have some phrases, and I can pull a leg or two when I'm in Wales, but no more than that. I'd like to have spoken the language well.'

Barry, born in 1942 and brought up on the Wirral, got a scholarship to Birkenhead School, and went to Liverpool University before getting a job in London. 'Then in 1967 Geoffrey Mason and I founded our own firm of chartered surveyors, and built a successful business in Liverpool.' Mason Owen is now the premier commercial surveyors on Merseyside, and one of only four provincial firms to be in Britain's top 50.

The Owen name traces back to Merionedd and to one Baron Owen. 'He was probably a bit of a pirate, controlling the Mawddach Estuary in the middle of the 16th century. He had 12 sons, and it is reckoned that most Owens have a connection through him,' says Barry.

His own family of six children are another generation away from the Merionedd connection; Barry's wife is Liverpool Irish. 'But my eldest daughter lives in Wales, so she is carrying on the Welsh tradition,' he says.

There have been a number of notable Owens connected to Liverpool, the most recent being Michael, Liverpool FC's star striker until 2004, when he accepted a transfer to Real Madrid, to the disgust of

The Owen name traces back to Merionedd and to one Baron Owen, who was probably a bit of a pirate, controlling the Mawddach Estuary in the mid 16th century

Red football fans everywhere.

Goronwy Owen and Wilfred Owen both made their mark on poetry. 'Black Goronwy of Anglesea' was born across the Menai Strait in 1722 and was curate of Walton parish for a couple of years, before sailing to America in 1757. Wilfred Owen, who spent his childhood in Birkenhead, died at the age of 25 in the trenches of Flanders field, leaving the best war poetry in English – poems such as *Anthem for doomed youth* and *Dulce et decorum est*.

Born in 1925, Alun Owen became one of the leading writers of 1960s television drama. Born on Anglesey, his family moved to Liverpool when he was eight. He was an actor for some years, then began writing radio scripts for the BBC. In 1964 Dick Lester hired Owen to write the screenplay for the Beatles film *A hard days' night*; the same year he wrote the book for Lionel Bart's musical *Maggie May*. Then it was a solid run of excellent TV drama, including a trilogy of plays for ATV, starring Sean Connery, Michael Caine, and Paul Scofield.

A famous name in Liverpool's high street for over 100 years was that of Owen Owen, the son of another Merionedd farmer, who came to Liverpool in 1868 and founded the shop that carried his name. He became a retail pioneer, the first to give staff a half day off each week, and the first to work a five day week.

On the night he arrived, he wrote in his diary: 'A few notes to guide me to the Harbour of Best Success... a) Rise very early, live well and very cheaply. 2) Be honest to my customers and just to my creditors. 3) Pay debts as soon as possible so as to owe no man. 4) Work myself. 5) Be civil to everyone. 6) Time being

The sun sets over the Clwydian Mountains, seen across the Dee estuary

money, waste none. 7) Do not frequent theatres, music halls, or anything to the neglect of business.'

In 1960, an Owen Owen customer noted: 'You'd go in there where you hesitated going into Bon Marché or Hendersons. It was more customer-friendly, working class. I didn't feel inferior going in there.'

Owen Owen lasted till the late 1990s, and until the mid 1980s it was still family-run. It changed hands three times in 10 years, and although it still has one Liverpool store, the name has changed.

A medical Welshman better known in America than in Wales or his chosen home of Liverpool was Hugh Owen Thomas, arguably the father of orthopaedics. His was a family of bone-setters from Anglesey; his father Evan Thomas had moved to Liverpool at 19. Hugh Owen, after his medical training in St Asaph, Edinburgh and London, set up his practice in Liverpool. His treatment of fractures and other bone disorders, detailed in his seminal work *Hip, Knee and Ankle*, used his invention of rigid steel splints, which were manufactured in his own workshop. He also invented a wrench for the reduction of fractures, and an osteoclast to break and reset bones. The standard treatment of the time was amputation; the use of the Thomas splint reduced the mortality from compound fractures of the femur from 80% in 1916 to less than 8% in 1918 – 23 years after Thomas's death.

Music, of course, is in the blood of the Welsh. It was after the 1900 National Eisteddfod in Liverpool that the Liverpool Welsh Choral Union was founded, based on the 400-strong choir formed for the Eisteddfod. Now one of Britain's leading choral societies, it has 160 singing members and is closely associated with the Royal Liverpool Philharmonic orchestra.

The first conductor, Harry Evans, was one of the finest choir trainers in the country; Edward Elgar became a vice president of the Union, and after the war, Malcolm Sargent became principal conductor.

The same Celtic spirit that feeds the muse fuels the political soul of the Welsh, who have turned out a few firebrands, whether they speak from a soapbox or a pulpit. A major political catalyst to have a long-term effect on Wales's history was the decision in 1957 to site a reservoir near Bala to supply water for the city of Liverpool. The City Council decided to drown 800 acres of land in the Tryweryn valley – including the village of Capel Celyn with its school, post office, chapel and cemetery, and 12 farms.

There was bitter opposition from the 70 people who were to be displaced, backed by Welsh MPs and prominent personalities including Megan Lloyd George. Demonstrations, petitions, protests in Liverpool – all failed to block the scheme; Liverpool MP Bessie Braddock said: 'Everyone deplores the fact that some people must suffer, but that is progress.' Three attempts to sabotage the building of the dam resulted in prison sentences for the saboteurs. Celyn Lake was opened in 1965 by Liverpool's Lord Mayor, to a chorus of protest by the Free Wales Army, dressed openly in military uniform. With a new road built from Bala to Ffestiniog to replace the drowned road, the cost of Liverpool's new reservoir – the biggest dam in Wales – was £20 million.

Tryweryn is credited with boosting the popularity of Plaid Cymru – the nationalist party gained its first seat the year after the dam was opened. Some argue that the scandal of Tryweryn was the catalyst for setting up the Welsh Office, and ultimately the Welsh Assembly. All to give Liverpudlians some clean Welsh water.

Italy

Frank Santangelli

Liverpool's Italian community is fiercely proud of its origins, and although most of Little Italy has gone to the bulldozer the spirit of Little Italy persists in the descendants of the settlers of a century ago.

Even though he doesn't speak a word of Italian, and sounds like a thorough-going Scouser, Frank Santangelli is a proud advocate of his heritage. He lives in Kent Street, which crosses the Ropewalks, near Chinatown, but he and his eight siblings were brought up in Russell Street, off London Road. The oldest child, Frank speaks proudly of his mother Rosie, who died of cancer aged 50, over 20 years ago. 'My mum had three jobs: she was barmaid at the Roscoe Arms, she was a cleaner at India Buildings, and a domestic in the Women's Hospital in Catherine Street.' Frank's younger sister Angela also died of cancer, aged just 36.

Frank's great-grandfather Rafael came with his family to Liverpool in the first decade of the 20th century. 'I don't know why the Santangellis left Italy, but I assume they wanted to go to America.

'They stopped in Brighton for a couple of weeks, then they ran out of money and found their way to Liverpool. Some of the family stayed on the boat to New York.'

Frank pulls a paperback from the bookshelf and leafs through the pages till he finds a marker. It is *The Godfather* by Mario Puzo, and the marked passage mentions a New York congressman, Alfredo Santangelli. A real figure in history, Frank says, and a distant relation. 'All the Santangellis are related – we all come from this one village in Italy, near Naples.'

The Santangelli family established itself in Liverpool, in what became known as Little Italy – the cobbled streets and squares off Scotland Road that from 1880 saw a steady influx of Italian immigrants: Gerard, Hunter, Whale, Circus and Lionel Streets. By 1913 there were about 400 Italian born settlers in the area, and by 1920 the close-knit community had become an integral part of Liverpool life.

As a resident describes it: 'In the 1920s, on a sunny Sunday morning, Gerard Street resembled a scene from a typical little Italian town, with caged birds chirping in the streets, the sound of violins and mandolins, and the mouthwatering smell of traditional Italian food being cooked.'

The settlers earned a living as knife-grinders, musicians, organ-grinders and street entertainers. Some worked in hotels, some worked on the docks; some families, like the Gianellis, opened fish and chip shops. Gianelli's shop was open for 80 years and had the reputation as the best chip shop in Liverpool, even supplying 1950s stars appearing at the Empire Theatre such as Frankie Laine, Johnny Ray and Russ Conway.

Rafael Santangelli built up a successful ice cream business, starting in Gerard Street with a hand cart he pushed around the streets. His was one of several famous ice cream family businesses in Liverpool, along with well-known names like Podesta, Chiappe and Fusco.

Later Rafael invested in tricycle ice-cream carts, and as the business grew, introduced motorised vans. Rafael then moved the business to a former pub building on the corner of Gerard Street and Bennett Street, and began to distribute ice cream further afield. By the 1930s, the Santangelli ice cream company was the largest mobile ice cream vendor in the area, and their ice cream vans were a

Caged birds chirping in the streets, the sound of violins and mandolins, and the mouthwatering smell of traditional Italian food being cooked

The Regatta Storica on the centre of Venetian life: the Gran Canale

familiar sight in the streets of Liverpool.

'My grandad Francis was about five when the family left Italy; he took over the ice cream business from Rafael.'

Frank's father was the only boy in his family, with three sisters. He had twin brothers, but they died as babies. Frank's dad was a renegade, and went his own way, not wanting to go into the family business and ending up as a docker; he died aged 59 at the end of the 1980s.

The family ice cream business melted in the heat of competition from the mass producers like Lyons Maid. 'That knocked out all the independents,' says Frank.

There is some story, he says, about his grandfather being a gambler and losing his business on Brighton beach. 'He lost lots of money, then lost his horse and cart. He walked away, then turned back and took his apron off and said "You might as well have that, too".'

Frank chuckles, being something of a gambler himself. He takes an almost professional approach to the dogs and horses, studying form with an expert eye and giving the bookies a run for their money.

'I haven't had a job since 1978. I worked for British Leyland, but the workforce voted to take the money and go. So I thought it was pointless taking a job when your own workmates sack you.'

Born in Liverpool in 1950, Frank has never been to Italy, nor does he speak a word of Italian – but he's learning now. 'My Dad was a Scouser, so I didn't grow up hearing Italian at home. I was fluent in Church Latin, though,' he says.

Frank was one of the first altar boys at the Catholic Cathedral, at the age of seven; 'you're not supposed to be an altar boy till you're nine,' he says. He was there for four years, before the new Cathedral was built, so the services were all in the 1930s Lutyens crypt.

Frank has been married twice, and has

four children: sons Russell and James, and daughters Francine (mother of granddaughter Fern) and Alexandra. Russell lives in London and has two kids; James is in Chester with his wife and son.

Frank admits that he doesn't see much of his children and it is clear from what he says that his relationship with his second wife is somewhat strained.

He talks more happily of the complex connections between Italian families in Liverpool, explaining how he is related to the famous featherweight boxer Dom Volante. 'The Volantes originally came from Milan, and Angie Volante, who married Francesco Santangelli in 1917, was Dom's sister,' says Frank.

Little Dom Volante was a local legend. Born in 1905 to parents Vincenzo and Marie, in a room over a stable in Gerard Street, he was one of 14 children. He turned professional in 1922, aged 17, and in 1930 went on a tour of the USA, winning four and drawing one in his five scheduled bouts. He topped the bill at Madison Square Gardens, fighting Harry Carlton in front of 18,000 fans in 'the greatest battle ever seen in the arena'.

When he retired from boxing, Dom worked in the gymnasium at Liverpool University, then joined Cunard to work as a gym instructor on board the *Britannic*, the *Mauretania* and the *Queen Mary*.

He died in 1982, aged 77, and the deep affection of Liverpudlians for this famous little fighter was demonstrated by the number of people who packed into the church for his memorial service.

Liverpool's Italian community is still close-knit and keen to keep its traditions and stories alive. Frank admits he is not much involved in the community, day to day, but his pride in his connections and interest in their history is obvious. He hopes to get out to Italy some day soon.

Ireland

Pauline Speak

Pauline's story is one that thousands of people would recognise. 'My mother's parents came here from Ireland – Newry, Co Down – so that my grandfather Patrick Rush could join the British Army and fight for the King in the Great War. They had got married when Patrick was only 16, and Polly was 19; it couldn't have been much before they came to England.'

Patrick was captured and held as a prisoner of war – but Pauline says the family has no details of what happened. 'It's such a shame we didn't take an interest much earlier – but you don't, do you?'

During his stint as a POW, Patrick contracted tuberculosis; the disease finally killed him in 1926, at the age of 28. They had four children, though, of which the eldest was Pauline's mother.

Polly Rush remarried and had another four children; her second husband was also Irish, and worked as a boss ganger on building sites. 'He was quite well paid, wore a suit and trilby to work.'

Pauline's father's parents, James and Elizabeth Grant, were English, or at least had both been born in Liverpool. 'There might have been a Scottish connection somewhere,' she says. 'They lived in appalling conditions, in the cellar of a big Victorian house in Grafton Street, overlooking the docks.'

James Grant died when Pauline was about five years old, so she doesn't remember much about him. 'My grandmother Elizabeth had had polio and was wheelchair bound.'

Pauline's Irish grandmother lived in the tenements of Caryl Gardens – demolished now – on the dock road about a mile from the Pier Head. 'She never owned a clock; said she didn't need one since if she needed to know the time she'd ask one of her 24 grandchildren to look out of the window at the Liver Clock.

'When some new building went up and blocked her view of the Liver Building, she was furious,' laughs Pauline.

She was born in January 1947 to Archie and Vera Grant, and was brought up with her brother Jimmy and sister Margaret in Cleopas Street, Dingle. 'We had an elder sister, Veronica, but she died when she was nine months old. My dad couldn't ever talk about her – not ever.'

Archie worked as a labourer at Dysons, the trailer manufacturer, so he didn't earn much. 'My mum had a hard life bringing us up, but I didn't realise that till I was older. We were poor, but everyone was poor, so we didn't know any different.

'And I know it's a cliché, but we were very happy. There was a great community spirit, and we didn't miss what we didn't have. No-one locked their front door – they were open all day, so we never came home from school to find ourselves locked out. We had no electric till I was 15; we'd wrap up the hot racks out of the oven and use them to warm the beds, and we slept under old coats to keep warm.'

Pauline laughs as she remembers a joke about a child shouting down to his mother that the coat had fallen off the bed. 'His mother is embarrassed because she has a visitor, and tells him later not to say they had coats on the bed. So the next night, the boy calls down again: "Mum, our Billy's pulled the arm off the eiderdown!"'

There was never any money, she says, but they never felt deprived. 'Mum was always at the pawn shop – she'd get Dad's suit out of hock on Friday so he could wear it at the weekend, then on Monday

I was told to say that I went to the Protestant school. But when they asked, I blurted out 'Our Lady of Mount Carmel' and got thrown out for being honest

back it would go.

'But we didn't stint on clothes. Every bank holiday we'd all get a complete new outfit: coat, shoes, dress, hat. They had to last, of course, so if we grew too fast we were in trouble. We'd go to the shops in London Road and there'd be the cheque man, who'd ask Mum if she wanted a £5 cheque or a £10 cheque, which she'd used to buy our clothes, and pay back at so much a week – half a crown, or 7s.6d., depending on how much you borrowed. I supposed people were always in debt, but it's how everyone lived.'

When Pauline passed her 11+ exam, her parents were really proud of her, but she got stick from the kids in the street, who called her a 'college pudding' when they saw her in uniform.

'We were a Catholic family, one of only two in the street, so I went to Our Lady of Mount Carmel school in Walton – it would take me an hour and 20 minutes on the bus, each way.'

Being Catholic could get you into hot water in a solidly Orange area like the Dingle, she remembers. 'My Dad wasn't bothered – he'd go out and get drunk with the Orange men on 12 July as well as St Patrick's Day on 19 March!'

Pauline remembers a dancing club near the house. 'I was told to say, if asked, that I went to the Protestant school. But when they asked where I went to school, I blurted out "Our Lady of Mount Carmel" and got thrown out for being honest.'

More memories, this time of food. 'My dad was a traditionalist. He'd get home from work for lunch at exactly 12.10pm, and for tea at 5.10pm, and he'd expect his meal on the table. And he expected a hot

Reflection on a lake
Ireland

meal, with meat. So Dad had steak, even if the rest of us did without.'

Pauline chuckles as she remembers one day when her mother was frying a bit of steak and onions. 'She was called outside for a minute, and the cat dragged the meat out of the pan and on to the floor, and was fighting the dog off it when Mum came back in. She just washed the steak and put it back in the frying pan and Dad was none the wiser.'

No-one had fridges in those days, and meat would go off quickly – sometimes before it left the shop. 'Sometimes you'd peel back a slice of bacon that you'd just bought, and there'd be maggots between the rashers.'

It's enough to turn you vegetarian. Pauline remembers vividly the day she realised what meat was. 'I was seven. I went with Mum to the butcher's in Mill Street; there was sawdust on the floor, and blood. I looked at these halved beef carcasses hanging in the shop, and it suddenly clicked that meat was dead animals. I ran out of the shop and threw up in the gutter, and it was a good year before Mum could force me to eat any meat. Even now I don't each that much of it.'

Pauline lived at home till she was 19. 'I got pregnant with my 18-year old boyfriend, but there was never any pressure from my parents to get married if I didn't want to, which was pretty unusual for the 1960s.' She did marry, though, and the marriage lasted for 10 years, by which time they had three sons: Gary, Stephen and Michael. They lived in Morecambe for the first three years, which Pauline hated. 'I missed Liverpool so much and travelled back for all my antenatal care – I was determined that my first child would be born in Liverpool.'

Pauline admits that her husband, a teacher, was violent. 'But I didn't tell anyone. The police didn't actually do any-

thing – in those days it was just a domestic, and they left you to get on with it.' After the divorce, Pauline got married again, to Roger Speak. Wed in 1978, they had two sons, David and Peter.

David had been born with brain damage after a placental disruption that nearly killed Pauline. 'He wasn't expected to live, but he did, and ended up going to university,' she says with enormous pride.

Having left school with few qualifications, Pauline went first to night school, then to Liverpool Poly, where she qualified as a social worker. 'At my first job interview I was asked why I wanted to work in the city. I was astonished by the question, as it had never occurred to me to work anywhere else. This was my city, these were my people, and I loved them.'

Pauline retired on medical grounds in 1998; her health had been poor for some time. Days before she retired, she was diagnosed with breast cancer. 'Since then I have had six operations for breast and skin cancer, but I look really healthy, so I get no sympathy!' she laughs. 'I'm a positive person and just get on with it.'

But she and her family were hit hard when in January 2004 the police came to the house and told her that her son David had died. He was 27. 'We were all devastated. I thought when my parents died that that was the worse loss I could feel. But it doesn't compare to losing a child. Nothing can prepare you for it, and you never get over it. Never.'

David had been really proud that his mother was to be one of the Faces of Liverpool. 'Although I am not outstanding I have Liverpool in my heart. I'm rather like Liverpool in a way – times have sometimes been hard, and I have many scars, but I am still full of fight.'

Argentina

Adriana Stewart

'My name is Adriana Noemi Stewart, I am 40 years old, and I was born in Buenos Aires. There I met my husband Graham; we decided to move to England, so I arrived in Liverpool in July 2000 to start a new life here.

'As my English was very poor I had to attend an English school, and after studying very hard I achieved a Cambridge proficiency certificate.

'At the beginning, life here was not easy for me at all, not only because of the language but also for its different culture,' she says. 'Last year, our daughter Abigail was born here in Liverpool and since then my whole world has changed for good. I hope she will take the best from her parents' culture and of course be able to speak both English and Spanish.

'Anyway, I love challenges, and this is still one of my biggest.'

Buenos Aires, where Adriana was born in 1964, is a city of three million people, with a further nine million living in the greater metropolitan area around it. Stretching along the southern side of the Rio de la Plata (River of Silver) – or as we know it, the River Plate – the city is the gateway to Argentina. On the northern shore of the huge river delta, and due east of Buenos Aires, is Montevideo, capital of Uruguay.

A very European city, the influences of the Spanish, Italian and French colonisers are clear to see in the architecture, and in the fire and formality of the national dance, the tango.

To the southwest of the city stretches the Pampas, the vast flat plains which are Argentina's agricultural heartland and the home of the *gaucho* (cowboy). The location of Argentina's famous beef and grain industry, this is the source of the country's wealth. The area is dotted with small agricultural towns, which are home to the majority of Argentina's population, but hold little to interest the tourist.

> Not content with the way the Welsh settlers had been assimilated into the Argentine culture by 1902, some 230 Welsh left Patagonia from Port Madryn, on the Orissa; they sailed back to Liverpool and took ship for Canada

But sightseeing was far from the minds of the Liverpool-born Vestey brothers, sent by their father to investigate the potential of Argentina's economy. Their grandfather Samuel Vestey had been a provisioner in Liverpool, then the family specialised in butchery and became a pioneer of refrigeration technology; Union Cold Storage opened in Liverpool in 1897 to provide meat for the working class.

The Vestey brothers began importing meat from Argentina at the turn of the century, buying large cattle ranches to feed their processing plant in the Buenos Aires docks, the Anglo Frigorifico. This factory, at the height of its success, was processing 5,000 head of cattle per day; the carcasses were exported as chilled beef, and the hides, offal and insulin for

The Vestey brothers imported meat from Argentina, buying large cattle ranches to feed their processing plant with up to 5,000 head of cattle per day

Ushuaia – Tierra del Fuego's capital – the southern-most city in the world
Argentina

diabetics were valuable by-products.

To ship the beef, the Vesteys founded the Blue Star Line in 1911, and built a fleet of refrigerated ships with capital of £100,000.

In 1915, fed up with paying a huge tax bill, the brothers moved to Buenos Aires. By 1930 the Vestey Group had 30,000 employees worldwide, with interests in Brazil, Venezuela and Australia. During the war, though, the Blue Star Line would lose 29 ships and 646 crew members; the *Doric Star* was sunk by the infamous battleship *Graf Spee*.

After the war, Vesteys built a new fleet, including the *Argentina Star*, to carry 68 passengers as well as a cargo of beef in the refrigerated hold, from the UK to Rio de Janeiro, Montevideo and finally Buenos Aires. The seven week trip would include tying up at Dock Sud for seven days while the cargo was loaded.

Blue Star was not the only shipping company to run to Argentina, of course. Liverpool company Lamport & Holt ran the River Plate Steam navigation Company – formed in 1865 – and the Argentine Steam Lighter Company, owned from Liverpool but based in Buenos Aires, ran a fleet of feeder ships up and down the River Plate.

Alfred Booth & Co were running ships to Brazil and the Amazon: in the 1940s both Booths and Lamport & Holt were bought by Blue Star.

One of the odder connections between Liverpool and Argentina is the Spanish speaking country's Welsh speaking bit of Patagonia.

In May 1865 the *Mimosa* set sail in Liverpool, bound for the Atlantic coast of Patagonia. Aboard were 153 Welsh emigrants; today their descendants number about 25,000. The migration was led by a Welsh nonconformist minister, Michael D Jones, who had realised that by the second generation, Welsh emigrants in America were losing their language and national identity. Patagonia seemed to be a place on which Jones and his band of settlers could make an impact and keep their culture intact.

It was on 28 July 1865 that the *Mimosa* reached Gulf Nuevo in Chubut. From there they moved on to the Chubut river valley, where they set up a village called Rawson, now the capital city of the Chubut province.

The local Tehuelches helped the settlers get established, trading with them and taking part in each others' traditions. But despite the welcome from the locals and the government, hunger and disease took an early toll; within two years only 90 settlers survived in what the Welsh called Y Wladfa: the colony. They struggled on and eventually thrived. By 1914, when the migrations ended, about 3,000 Welsh people had come to Patagonia.

The Argentine government tried to eradicate the Welsh language, and managed to make Spanish the dominant tongue; but in the early 1990s Welsh language became fashionable, and has made a comeback.

The annual Chubut Eisteddfod started in 1875 – a hybrid Welsh-Spanish festival of poetry and music.

Not content with the way the Welsh settlers had been assimilated into the Argentine culture by 1902, 230 Welsh left Patagonia from Port Madryn, on the Orissa; they sailed to Liverpool and took ship for Canada, settling in Llewellyn, Cymric and Glaslyn, Saskatchewan.

Tradition runs strong in Patagonia, even now. As Chubut's tourist office puts it: 'The Welsh tea, the home-made bread and cakes, and the secrets about the famous 'black pudding' are all well kept in each of the homes of Welsh descent.'

South Africa

Shirley Mashiane Talbot

Shirley Mashiane Talbot arrived in Liverpool in 1969, from South Africa via Oxford. She was brought up near Pretoria, in a very segregated area of South Africa. One of nine children, the family shared a four-roomed house next door to the clinic where her mother worked as a nurse and midwife.

'It was a very difficult time – we would see lots of domestic servants who had been raped by their employers,' she remembers. 'We played with white children, even though our schooling was segregated and we knew it was illegal. They were usually the children of doctors, or people who were working with my mother. I was very angry and for a while had a real hatred of white people for what they were doing to us. I was sent to a Catholic boarding school – it was the best place to be – away from the townships, and all the crime and police interference there.'

Shirley was 15 when she first joined the ANC (African National Congress). 'I didn't really understand much, and I didn't do much, but a group of students came round door-to-door and I joined.' Following in her mother's footsteps, Shirley took up nursing, and it was then that she became more involved in the ANC and started working with the underground.

'We were near the university; Mandela was there and it was a politically fertile time. The nurses had been on strike before I arrived and we started helping the students who had been arrested.'

As things became tougher in South Africa, students were rounded up and imprisoned in increasing numbers. Shirley was advised to go into exile; she applied for a course that wasn't available in South Africa and used it as a passport out of the country. Ironically, nurses and religious people – where there was a lot of anti-apartheid activity – weren't being clamped down on, and were given a 10% discount on travel.

'Lots of people left the country after Sharpeville in 1960.' The Sharpeville Massacre saw 69 black Africans killed and between 200 and 300 injured as they protested against the introduction of new pass laws. It signified the beginning of armed resistance in South Africa and the date, 21 March, is marked by South Africa's Human Rights Day.

Shirley continues: 'It wasn't only the ANC, but the Pan Africanist Movement and the trade unionists. The laws really started clamping down, and at the same time the Anti-Apartheid Movement was starting in the UK, partly because of the number of people fleeing South Africa for England. But the English people linked up and publicised apartheid and formed the solidarity movement.'

Shirley left in 1965. Her passport came through four days before she was due to leave the country and she left immediately, knowing the authorities would then check her passport against police records. She took a boat to England, which took 21 days (the sea journey now takes under two weeks; by air it is just ten hours).

'I was the only African on the boat – there were some Indians – and the white people were very cautious. We had some fun: we'd wait until they were all in the swimming pool before we got in. Then we'd watch them make their excuses and all get out again.' But, as they approached Britain, attitudes mellowed.

By 1967 she had gained a place at

The white people on the boat were very cautious. We'd wait until they were all in the swimming pool before we got in. Then we'd watch them make their excuses and get out again

Ruskin College in Oxford, studying for a Diploma in Social Studies. France saw huge protests at the Sorbonne university in 1968, and Oxford too was starting to become very active. She knew fellow South African Peter Hain – now the Chairman of the Labour Party – well at the time. Shirley would get up at the crack of dawn every morning to emblazon the latest bulletin of the struggle on the college's walls. Oxford was a significant place to be at the time: 'Lots of people who are now in the South African government were studying there at the time. People there were politically active.'

Moving to Liverpool, in 1969, she walked straight into a protest. 'Students were protesting about Rhodesia and completely took over Senate House.' They were led by Channel 4's newsreader Jon Snow, who was promptly ejected from the university for his trouble. And it was here that Shirley met her husband. 'I met my husband in Liverpool. He'd just started his first job after finishing at Cambridge, and was a socialist – a music lecturer. We married after about nine months – he's British, and in those days I became a British subject automatically.'

Arriving in Liverpool, Shirley continued to work in and campaign for women's issues and multi-racial education, even taking the chair of the ANC's Women's Section. 'Liverpool was the best place for me to come as an activist. There was a bedrock of support here. Lots of places were getting rid of colonialism and Liverpool had lots of connections with them – particularly in West Africa – and a history of working with black Americans. It was the early 1970s, industry was run-

ning down, the trade unions were very active and there was lots of solidarity, especially from the dockers and sailors, many of whom carried messages for us into South Africa.'

The South African community in Liverpool at the time was very small, but was characterised, says Shirley, by 'some outstanding people, like Professor Hendrix, the director of the Liverpool School of Tropical Medicine.'

Working in education, Shirley pushed for more inclusive education, and was one of the first to start courses in Afro-Caribbean studies in the city. 'There was still lots of resistance, but we started to look at a lot of American writing. I just wanted to permeate the syllabus. Make it more rounded, more diverse. Slowly I was getting to know the black community here. They have contributed a lot to our struggle. I will never forget the immense support of Liverpool people.

'The 1980s were a really grim time for us in terms of a way forward. Three black elders from the Afro-Caribbean Asian Association invited me for some food, and said: "We don't know which way things are going, and we want to adopt you." It really touched me. It was all about bringing black people together.'

Liverpool, of course, had problems of its own through the 1970s and 1980s. Images of rioting in Toxteth still scar the national consciousness. 'I think the uprisings showed the conditions for black people here. It showed the problems and pricked the consciousness. It was hard for people to get mortgages, and jobs, and if you went into town there were hardly any black faces. I remember coming out of what used to be George Henry Lee and the police were piling black people into the back of a van. They nearly put me in there, just because I was black. That stayed with me for a long time.

'Liverpool has a huge number of racially mixed families, but there were hardly any black people in the police. Relations with the police still aren't easy, but now they are doing as much as they can to involve the communities and recruit black officers. There's a long way to go though; there's still a lot of hurt, anger and pain there.'

It was 25 years before Shirley returned to South Africa. 'My mother came over every four years – we always bought her a ticket, but one December, just after Mandela was released, my family just said "go home".'

On top of her work in Liverpool, Shirley maintains her ties with her homeland through the work she does with the Joseph Rowntree Charitable Trust and the Canon Collins Educational Trust, and visits more regularly now – sometimes for work, sometimes for pleasure. 'I missed it very much when I couldn't go back,' she admits. 'I missed the warmth of the people – although I have found a lot of that in Liverpool – and I missed the food and the weather. But I didn't miss the creepy crawlies or the thunder.'

One of the problems South Africa faces right now – like many of the African nations – is the brain drain of skilled workers moving to the UK and US, often in search of higher wages. 'A lot of people went back, and then a lot of people left again. Some have gone back since. But South Africa has a lot going for it, especially if it can tackle the HIV and Aids problem (Shirley is a trustee of Sahir House here in Liverpool, which works with Aids sufferers, their families and carers), and the unemployment problem. It's only been ten years, which is not a lot of time really. There is still a lot to be done.'

Malaysia

Julien Hock Toh

Born in 1995 in Liverpool, Julien Hock Toh is five generations away from his roots in Fujian, China. Half his roots, at least – his mother Christine comes from Normandy, France.

Julien's father, Cheng-Hock Toh, was born in Malaysia to third generation economic migrants from Fujian, growing up in Ipoh, capital of Perak province and until the 1970s the centre of Malaysia's huge tin industry.

'My father remembers his parents being worried about being Chinese in Malaysia, and also about the idea that communism would spread from mainland China down through South East Asia,' he says.

Fujian, now with a population of 25 million, was the most secluded province of China: mountainous and thickly forested, it didn't get its first railway line until the mid 1950s. Still, there has been a strong academic tradition in the province, and in the Chinese Academies of Science and Engineering there are more members from the capital Fuzhou than from any other city. Rich in mineral deposits and very fertile, Fujian is famous for its Wuyi Mountain tea, and the Pingtan area produces excellent laver – a seafood delicacy that some say is what the Liver Birds hold in their beaks.

Perak, in the north of Peninsular Malaysia, is the second largest state in the country. The name Perak means silver in Malay, referring to the silvery tin ore mined there. The state produced the world's largest supply of tin until the industry collapsed 30 years ago.

> I find these endeavours equally rewarding, not only in bridging philosophical themes common to medicine, science and the arts, but also in justifying professional and personal responsibilities to society

The rich mineral deposits attracted a series of colonists, ending with the Dutch and the British in the 19th century swapping control until 1826, when British rule came in to stay till 1941 and the Japanese invasion. The British did get Malaya back after the war, but local patriotism fuelled a drive for independence, which came about in 1957.

The growing importance of tin in the world market in the 19th century brought an influx of Chinese immigrants into the rich minefields of Larut.

In the early 1870s the British used the happy coincidence of a row over Malay royal succession and the battles of two secret Chinese societies known as Ghee Hin and Hai San, who constantly waged battle against each other for control of the tin mines in Perak. The British backed one of the royal princes and promised to sort out the Chinese feud, in return for covert British control of Larut.

The British Resident, whose 'advice' was to be taken by the Raja, was JWW Birch, but in 1875 Birch was assassinated by a group of Malay chieftains. In Ipoh

There is a memorial to Birch – the Ipoh Clock Tower. And on the spot where he was actually killed, there is another memorial, but this one is dedicated to the Malays who killed him

The still waters of Langkawi, Malaysia

there is a memorial to Birch – the Ipoh Clock Tower, opposite the splendid railway station. And on the spot where Birch was actually killed, there is another memorial, but this one is dedicated to the Malays who killed him.

The Malaysian Chinese people are fiercely protective of their ethnic identity and intermarriage with native Malays is fairly rare due to the factor of Islam. Most Malaysian Chinese consider their being Chinese both a political and an ethnic identity. They have traditionally dominated the Malaysian economy, but with the introduction of affirmative action policies by the Malaysian government, their share has been somewhat eroded, although they still make up the majority of the middle and upper income classes of Malaysia.

The day after Federal elections in 1969, simmering racial tension between Malays and Chinese boiled over, and riots broke out in Kuala Lumpur. The violence resulted in hundreds of deaths and damage to property. It took four days to restore order, but localised violence continued to break out over the next two months, only stopping when the government threatened severe action against the militant Malay groups.

Such incidents can have done nothing to reassure Julien's grandparents, and by the mid-1970s they had persuaded Cheng-Hock that a professional career, preceded by an English education, would be a sensible way forward.

'He had to choose between being a doctor and being an artist,' says Julien, 'and in the end the doctor won.'

Cheng-Hock arrived in England in 1978, heading for public school and A levels – boarding school being 'a somewhat alien environment', as he puts it.

After A levels, he went to Sheffield where he qualified as a doctor in 1985. Further medical training in Manchester

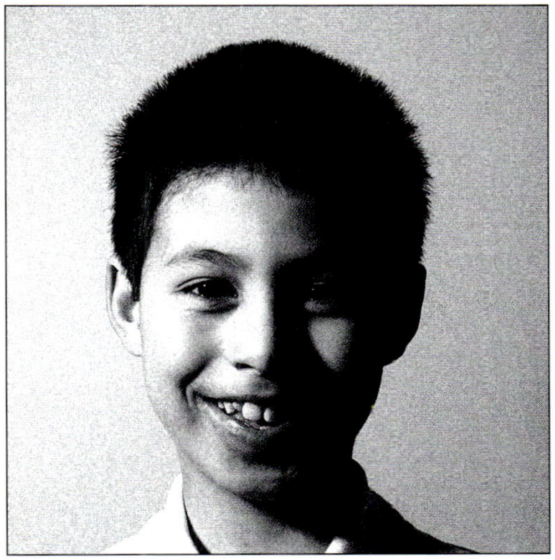

and Newcastle followed, then Cheng-Hock went to Ontario to pursue research into heart disease and strokes.

It was in Canada that he met his wife, Christine. They married in Canada, and Julien was born in 1995, within four weeks of arriving in Liverpool.

Cheng-Hock had been appointed consultant haemotologist at the Royal Liverpool University Hospital. Julien lets his father explain his work.

'I'm also a Reader at the University of Liverpool with research and teaching commitments,' says Cheng-Hock.

'Whilst my direct patient contact is in the highly specialised area of bleeding and excessive clotting conditions, I also have a public health role in steering the group that guides general practitioners in Liverpool on aspects of stroke prevention.'

A large grant from a charitable foundation funded the creation of the Roald Dahl Haemotosis and Thrombosis Centre at the Royal, opened in 2001.

'The Centre has received local, national and international recognition, especially in its research output that now includes a patent for novel diagnostic testing in the critically ill patient,' says Cheng-Hock with justifiable pride.

Alongside its core work in collaborating with international scientists, the Roald Dahl Centre works with local artists. 'We want both to improve the visual environment in the hospital, and to translate this area of clinical science for the public.'

Still with a passionate interest in the creative and performing arts, Cheng-Hock found time to curate an exhibition for the Bluecoat Crafts Display Centre.

'I find these endeavours equally rewarding, not only in bridging philosophical themes common to medicine, science and the arts, but also in justifying professional and personal responsibilities to society.'

Norway

Michael Vangen

Ask a Scouser to name three famous Norwegians and they'd probably come up with John Arne Riise, Thomas Myhre and Noggin the Nog. What they may not know is that Liverpool has a significant Scandinavian community of Norwegians, Swedes, Danes, Finns and Icelanders. All of them seafaring nations, of course, so there have been links between Norsemen and Scousers for longer than Liverpool has existed. Viking blood still courses through veins on Merseyside, some of it through Michael Vangen, courtesy of his father Johan, an officer in the Royal Norwegian Navy who was posted to Liverpool in 1941, met local girl Marjorie and married her.

Johan survived the war, despite being on Atlantic convoys and minesweepers; during a year's posting in Dundee, their son Michael was born in 1944.

After the war, the family went back to Norway, and for his first few years, Michael grew up on the family's farm outside Tromsø, on Norway's west coast, north of the Arctic Circle. The Vangen family was extensive – Johan was one of 10 siblings, so Michael had numerous aunts, uncles and cousins.

In the days of Michael's grandparents, the farm kept them mostly self-sufficient, and their main income came from fishing. 'When my father was small, he was still expected to do his bit, helping to load up barrels of herring and cooking for the ship's crew.'

Even when Michael went to boarding school at Rossall, near Fleetwood, he spent up to six weeks every summer back in Tromsø. And later, when Michael settled in Liverpool, the Norwegians often came for long visits. 'We have always kept in close contact,' he says. 'We've just had five of them to stay with us.'

Michael and Linda's two children – both grown up – are not as close to the Norwegian culture as their father. 'They enjoy the connection, and come for the high days and holidays, but they were born in Liverpool and don't feel the pull as much as I still do.'

When Michael's father left the Navy after the war, the family came back to Liverpool – his mother's home. The couple set themselves up in the fashion business and built a small chain of shops – Cherry's Boutique des Enfants (later the shops sold ladies' fashions too). Marjorie loved the buying, and her fashion sense had the women of Liverpool flocking for colour and style after the austerity of the war. 'They could really compete – even with the big stores – throughout the 1950s and into the 1960s,' says Michael.

Michael went to university in Toronto, and loved his four years in Canada, although in those days, he says, 'it was quite an austere Presbyterian city, not the cosmopolitan place it is now.' He qualified as a chiropracter in 1970, and set up his practice in Liverpool – the first, and still the only member of the British Chiropractic Association in the city.

He and his wife Linda go back to Norway as often as they can – usually two or three times a year. They still have the farm, and the family works hard to maintain the farming traditions.

Tradition is strong in the Vangen household here in Liverpool, too. 'We enjoy Norwegian food, of course,' says Michael with a grin. 'A special favourite is *geitost*, a sweet brown goat's cheese. And we often make waffles – which is a Norwegian spe-

The two places have much in common, with their connections reaching back over 1,000 years and with veins full of sea salt and Viking genes

The fishing village of Moskenesoya, Sakrisoya Island
Norway

ciality. When you visit a house there you will often be given strong black coffee, waffles and jam.'

A lot of Norwegian cuisine is based around fish, unsurprisingly – cod, herring, shrimp, salmon – and it figures strongly in the traditional Christmas menu.

And of course food is another link with Liverpool – it was Scandinavian sailors who brought the dish Lobscouse to Liverpool and turned us into Scousers.

For Scouse Scandinavians, it must be a comfort to know that a supply of special Nordic groceries is kept at the Scandinavian church on Park Street, which is the heart of the community in Liverpool. The church – often known as the Swedish Seaman's Church of Gustav Adolph, was built to minister to the needs of Scandinavian seamen while in the port, a haven where they could meet their countrymen, get advice on all sorts of matters, spiritual and otherwise, and feel at home in a foreign port.

The 1882 Sjomanskyrkan is based on a traditional Norwegian stavkirche (a design that dates back to Viking times), but built in red glazed brick rather than timber.

Today, the church is still very much at the heart of the community. Thursday is the social evening; Norwegian language classes are held there. And everyone is welcome for lunch on Wednesdays.

His childhood home of Tromsø has some features in common with Liverpool. With a population of 60,000, it is much smaller, but it is a university town, and has more bars per capita than anywhere else in the country, and the liveliest nightlife. Like Liverpool, the town is dominated by two churches: the wooden Domkirke, and the magnificent Ishavskatedralen, or the Arctic Cathedral. Built in the 1960s, its 11 spires and stained glass reflect the glaciers and peaks of the Arctic landscape. And of course there are

ferries crossing the water to the little islands just offshore.

To see a little bit of Norway in Liverpool, head for the Pier Head on 17 May, which is Norway's National Constitution Day. The entire community turns out to celebrate, says Michael. 'We congregate at the Pier Head, with a band, and a police escort, and all flags waving; we march up James Street, down Lord Street, and along Paradise Street to the Seamen's church. Then we have a party – weather permitting – in the garden behind the church in Cornhill.'

The active community is about 1500 strong, although there are far more of Scandinavian descent, second, third or even fourth generation Liverpudlians. Not to mention the Viking throwbacks.

Norwegians are independent people, and proud of their country, with some justification. With 95% of the country uninhabitable – lakes, mountains, tundra and glaciers – the 4.5 million Norwegians have a booming economy, with wealth per capita on a level with the USA. Huge wealth from oil and gas, hydroelectric power generation, a massive merchant fleet, big fishing industry, ship building, telecoms, and a huge tourist industry. 'Not surprisingly, Brussels wants Norway in the EU,' says Michael. 'But in two referenda the people said no to Europe.'

Now Europe has awarded Stavanger, Norway's oil town, the status of non-EU Capital of Culture in 2008, alongside Liverpool as the EU European Capital. How well the two cities will succeed in sharing the title, only time will tell. But if Liverpool's Nordic community is anything to go by, the two places have much in common, with their connections reaching back over 1,000 years and with veins full of sea salt and Viking genes. Too good an opportunity to waste.

China

Stephen Yip

Since 1975, Stephen Yip has been working flat out for the children of Liverpool, raising millions of pounds for the charity he founded: Kids in Need and Distress. In 2005 KIND is 30, and Stephen is 50. Big anniversaries – but Stephen seems to have as much energy now as he did when he was 20. He certainly doesn't talk any slower; the rapid fire conversation suggests that he has better things to do than talk about himself, such as packing 7,000 hampers for children whose families can't afford Christmas.

One of ten children, Stephen's surname comes from his father, who was from Canton; his mother was English. 'My dad left home when he was a child: he was 13 when he went to sea, and although he went back to China often, he never went home again.

'He would never talk about his family or his childhood; we'd pick up hints from things he said, but we never found out anything much except that it was hard – not having enough to eat was an incentive to find work on a ship. He'd have done all kinds of work on board, from stoker to cook, and although the Chinese crews were paid a fraction of the wages of a British seaman, it was better than starving.

'There were no birth certificates in China when he was born, so we didn't know his exact birthdate; he left China in the early 1900s, so was coming up to 90 when he died ten years ago.'

When Loy Yip first came to Liverpool, he stayed where everyone else stayed, around Pitt Street and Cleveland Square. 'It was a Little Peking, old Chinamen with pigtails and all that. There were Africans, some Indians, Yemenis – the local school was known as the League of Nations.

'Everybody got on fine round there, but there was a lot of racism in the city, of course. Signs in windows saying "No Chinese, No Dogs".

'I don't think the Chinese have ever been appreciated in Liverpool. It's a quiet community, and their input has never been properly recognised.'

Loy met Stephen's mother in Liverpool, and they were typical of generations of couples – foreign seamen marrying English women and settling here with a family that the mothers would bring up while their husbands were away at sea.

Loy Yip worked for the Blue Funnel line, the Liverpool shipping line founded by Albert and Philip Holt. With Homeric names like *Ajax* and *Agamemnon*, the distinctive ships had Chinese crews and British officers.

'These were long haul ships to the Far East and China; Dad would be away for several months at a time, then home for a month. It must have been hard to settle into a home routine, for both my parents. Of course we kids were spoilt rotten when Dad came home, and we all remember getting exotic presents. He'd bring back toys from China, like the first robots that walked, and tin ships that powered themselves round the bath. And fireworks. And food.'

His father kept chickens in the cellar and would kill them for the pot. 'We used to love watching these headless chickens running round the cellar, blood going everywhere.' he says.

'I've been vegetarian for 15 years now. Dad couldn't understand it at all – he'd eat absolutely anything and couldn't understand why I wouldn't eat meat.'

The family lived, in the late 1950s and

We were spoilt rotten when Dad came home. He'd bring back toys from China, like the first robots that walked, and tin ships that powered themselves round the bath. And fireworks

The frozen lakes of the Summer Palace
Beijing, China

early 1960s, in Duke Terrace – the last back-to-backs in Liverpool. 'You couldn't wish for a better place to live,' says Stephen. 'Nine houses round a courtyard that you got to up an entry. You could play out, with eight sets of neighbours to look out for you in your private playground. We did have indoor loos, but no hot water.

'And we were two minutes from everywhere – up to the Cathedral, down to Pier Head, over to Bold Street, which in those days was the premier shopping street.'

Loy and Betty moved to Duke Terrace after the war, and had ten children, of whom eight survived. 'Seven boys and a girl – Graham is a superintendent in Merseyside Police, David is an actor living in Oxford, Brian works for British Airways and lives in Brighton, and the others live fairly local – Peter, Paul, Michael and Doreen.'

It must have been hard, especially for his mother, struggling to bring up eight kids, but Stephen remembers a very happy childhood.

He has never moved far from that first home. Up the hill a bit, he has lived in Hope Place for 24 years; at No14 for most of that time, and now in the old Convent of Notre Dame.

Stephen has two grown-up daughters, but he and his wife now have a one-year old baby which, he admits, is a challenge, albeit a lovable one.

Then there are the thousands of kids who have been through the doors of KIND over the years. Stephen and his team run residential weeks for up to 600 kids a year, for some time on KIND's Scottish estate. 'But it cost us £600,000 a year to run that place. It was fantastic for the kids, but it was too far, and too expensive. So we sold it, and now run weeks in the Lake District.' The point of the residential weeks is to show children that

there are other possible ways to live, and other realities to the one they're used to. Even a week is enough to have a positive effect on their lives, as he has proved time and again.

'We get a variety of kids, but the problems haven't changed much in 30 years; there's still a lot of deprivation in the city.'

In 1998 KIND opened its City Environment Centre, tucked away in Back Canning Street where you wouldn't imagine there was room for a window box. 'We can take 3,000 schoolchildren through the centre every year; they can learn so much, from growing and gathering food plants and looking after animals like our rabbits, to wildlife habitats. We have a pond in the garden full of newts and frogs, so the kids can go pond-dipping. All in the shadow of the Cathedral.'

He has exciting plans for the 30th anniversary. It is all in the early stages of feasibility studies, but Stephen has his fingers crossed to get a new centre built in Liverpool in time for 2008. 'For 29 years we have taken kids out of Liverpool – so what about having our own centre in Liverpool? Now that the city has changed so dramatically, and for the better, I want to use all the cultural stuff we have – all the amazing things the kids could do.'

Liverpool has always been a city of change, he says. 'Waves of incomers, all with their own ways of doing things, all adding to the rich Scouse pot.'

World events dictate who turns up, he suggests, from Cypriots and Ugandan Asians in the 1970s to Congolese and Kosovans fleeing from war in the late 1990s. 'It's the kids who turn into Scousers; within a year they sound like everyone else while their parents struggle to learn the language. But that's how integration works; it's the next generation that embraces the local culture.'

HONORARY

Hungary

Andrew Zsigmond

The civilised surroundings of Rodney Street consulting rooms – which are also the offices of the Hungarian Consulate for the North of England – are a long way from bloody revolt in 1950s Budapest, but a Liverpool doctor is the link.

Born near the Transylvanian town of Tîrgu Mures in 1935, Andrew Zsigmond, Baron de Lemhény, was a 21 year old medical student at Pécs University, in communist-ruled Hungary, when on 23 October 1956 a demonstration in the capital Budapest blew up into a full scale revolution in a matter of hours.

'I, like so many others, took up arms to arrest secret police and communist party officials and to resist the invading Red Army,' says Andrew. The hated AVO secret police were one of the first targets for the revolutionaries – it was when the AVO began firing into the crowd of protesters on 23 October that the crowd turned from protest to armed revolt.

Hungary had been under the iron fist of Joseph Stalin since the war, with Hungary's wealth siphoned off to Soviet Russia, and Soviet troops and tanks moved in to enforce Stalin's regime. After Uncle Joe's death in 1953 the Hungarians were hoping for better under the new Soviet leader Krushchev, but although he made a a few concessions to Hungarian demands, it was not enough.

The popular uprising saw up to 100,000 Hungarians in the streets, with students issuing their demands for more personal freedom, better food, the removal of the secret police, more democratic government, and so on.

On 4 November Soviet troops and tanks swept through Budapest, killing tens of thousands of rebels and wounding many thousands more. The suppression was brutal – troops were even dragging bodies through the streets as a warning to the rebels. Almost 200,000 refugees fled Hungary before the end of the year.

'As I was the editor of the extraordinary edition of the University Weekly, they came looking for me. I lay low in my father's cellar until my father urged me to leave the country. He knew what the options were – he had been a senior policeman in 1948 when the communists stuck him in jail for a couple of years.

'By the end of the year, most of the refugees had already fled; we had stayed almost too long. On 2 January 1957 a group of five of us left. As well as me, there was another medical student, his brother, a 65 year old actor who was the Errol Flynn of Hungary, and one other.

'In various disguises, we took the train as far it we could go, and then we had to walk the rest of the way to Austria. We walked at night and slept by day, and it took us three nights. It should have taken only two, but the terrain through the Austrian Alps was difficult – crevasses and ridges in deep snow; and then there was getting lost, and dogs...' He makes light of the journey.

'We had guns, but we threw them away because if we'd been armed when they caught us they would have shot us immediately. No guns, and we would only have been deported to Siberia.

'When we got to the border there was a bigger group ahead of us. They were heavily armed, and were spotted by the border guards. The shooting gave us cover, and we ran for it.'

So the little band reached the refugee camp in Austria on 5 January. Andrew

We had guns, but we threw them away because if we'd been armed when they caught us they would have shot us immediately. No guns, and we would only have been deported to Siberia

glosses over the horrors of the camp and moves the story on. 'Of all things, a red doubledecker London bus turned up – it was a recruiting office for the National Coal Board in Britain. We signed up, and by 13 January we'd been lifted out and were in Barnsley, as apprentice miners. We didn't speak a word of English, but the pay was good – £7.13s.6d.'

Barnsley didn't keep him for long; Andrew moved on to Wath-on-Dearne as a hospital ward orderly. He was determined to get back to his medical studies, and got the local MP, Roy Mason, to help him apply to Liverpool University for a place in the third year of a medical degree. 'The problem was my English.

'You couldn't buy an English-Hungarian dictionary, so I had to learn parrot-fashion. In the end, I managed to persuade the professor to allow the interview to be conducted in Latin, which I spoke much better than English.'

Liverpool looked very different in 1957; the damage inflicted in the war had left huge holes in the fabric of the city, and, he says, 'all those lovely buildings were pitch black. St George's Hall, the Three Graces, and worst of all, the Lyceum in Bold Street. The Lyceum was so bad that the colour was known as Lyceum Black.'

Andrew graduated in 1961, and, he says, that's the end of the story. Only chapter two, of course.

'University life was good, and to be in Liverpool in the 1960s was fantastic – it was the city's first renaissance.'

Having left politics behind for 35 years, Andrew got involved in the 1992 general elections, in this most political of cities, standing as a Tory candidate in the Riverside ward – one of the safest Labour

seats in the country. 'I did pretty well, coming second and beating the LibDems.

'But then I was kicked out of the Tory Party. I have the letter that says I'm no longer welcome.'

So what on earth had prompted this piece of uncivilised correspondence? 'I was too European for them. I stood as a pro-Europe Conservative candidate in the Euro elections, and they didn't like it.'

The following year he was appointed Honorary Consul of the Republic of Hungary; since then he has been president of the Liverpool Consular Corps.

In 2003 he was decorated by the President of Hungary for his part in the 1956 Revolution, and he is also an honorary General of the National Guards.

Having put aside his political interests, at least for now, Andrew is involved in a number of charitable organisations and some personal projects, including a major undertaking in Transylvania. He explains: 'The pastor of the village where I was born wrote to me, saying he had found my name in the baptismal register, and would I build a new church for him, please? I didn't answer the letter for a long time, and when I finally sat down to reply, feeling a little guilty that I planned to write that I wasn't up to building churches, I started typing and found that instead of saying no, I was saying yes.'

He laughs, proud of the splendid new Reformed Church of St Laszlo and the youth centre alongside it.

In the summer of 2004, Andrew went back to his birthplace, taking 40 members of his family with him, including some Hungarian relatives he had never met before. 'It was a fantastic family reunion.'

A splendid resumé of his career achievements includes being the civilian medical officer to the RAF, carrying out screenings and medicals for pilots, both military and civil. He specialises in occupational medicine, and is called on as an expert witness in court cases.

Andrew's consular duties have been fairly light until recently, with a small Hungarian population in Liverpool of perhaps 25 to 50 people. But since Hungary joined the EU this year, the workload has already increased. 'I am Honorary Consul for the area between Birmingham and Scotland,' he says. He is working, in his consular capacity, towards getting an agreement on close co-operation between the cities of Liverpool and Pécs, where he was at university. And there is already an exchange programme to bring doctors over to Liverpool to work at the Royal for a couple of years: 'there are always a few Hungarian doctors in A&E,' he says.

Between all this he has time to ski well, play golf badly, and listen to his enormous collection of opera records and CDs. 'My favourite opera is Verdi's *Otello.* I wouldn't be surprised if I had a better collection than the BBC – 45 complete box sets, plus highlights and arias.' Music is a great passion, and Andrew is quick to point out that the composer and virtuoso pianist Franz Liszt played twice in Liverpool, and that Bartok's Music for Strings was premiered at the Philharmonic Hall. 'in November [2004] I was down in London at the unveiling of a statue to Bartok.'

And what about the other four escapees from Russian reprisals after the uprising? 'One is a doctor in Liverpool, like me. The actor went to the USA and, having played one so often on stage, became a real life butler of such distinction that he became butler to Rockerfeller.'

Another of them, who also went to America didn't fare so well. 'He got a job as an animator with Walt Disney, but the memories of the past were too much for him, and he committed suicide three or four years after we left Hungary.'

connections

the people

From the outset, our vision as artists and designers was to create a space to accommodate people; a new public realm that could be successfully inhabited. It is a space that enlivens the senses, and evokes memory and imagination, as well as overcoming the physical difficulties of the site's extreme micro-climate and heavy traffic flow.

The life of the project is now so much bigger than its designers and makers. It is owned by the brave souls and their families, who agreed to tell their very personal stories of departure and arrival – the 'Faces of Liverpool'.

These faces have shared not only their image, but their life story for this and future generations, inspiring courage for both the alien and the community that welcomes their diversity. They have granted the stranger 'permission to come alongside'.

Michael O'Mahoney's 1931 quotation, 'Liverpool – threshold to the ends of the earth' sets the context and reason for the site's existence, both past and present – and itself forms an integral feature of the garden.

The site is indeed at the threshold of national and international connections... of arrivals and departure. The Terminal Basin canal cottages give visual evidence of a gateway to the east coast, along the Leeds-Liverpool canal; the adjacent Princes Dock is a western gateway to the New World. The new Passport Office and Radisson hotel also strengthen these international connections.

Sculptural elements integrated within the landscape make these connections, and evoke stories of travel, trade and adventure using simple geometry, symbols and maps. Throughout the whole scheme subtle intersecting lines, etched, cast, blasted, and illuminated – within walls and floorscape – link portholes that portray 32 Liverpool faces of the world.

These contemporary faces represent in some part Liverpool's diverse gene pool: pioneers, traders, travellers, migrant people, or visitors that simply stayed, throughout history, from all over the world. They are all people that have made Liverpool their home.

Stephen Broadbent, sculptor